"This book offers a transformative blend of personal story and practical advice. Lydia shares her journey in deeply personal and universally relatable ways, offering us insightful, actionable steps for our own growth. A beacon of hope and guidance."

Marci Shimoff, #1 NY Times bestselling author
Happy for No Reason and Chicken Soup for the Woman's Soul

"I hold Lydia's openness and candid vulnerability in a sacred space. Her willingness to share her story gives hope and leads towards courage. Lydia's insights are pure and serve as motivation to us all to move forward. A must read."

Lisa Garr, Host of *The Aware Show*,
Author of *Becoming Aware*

TO HELL WITH YOU

TO HELL WITH YOU

An Adventure Through
Tragedy, Love, Betrayal
and Transformation

Lydia Gascón Samaniego

Published by

GASCONIEGO
PUBLISHING

∞

lydiasamaniego.com

ISBN (paperback): 979-8-9911385-0-5
ISBN (ebook): 979-8-9911385-1-2

Book design and production by www.AuthorSuccess.com

Printed in the United States of America

To my four sons.
You are my reason for everything.
Thank you!

Table of Contents

Introduction

Have you ever felt that you have made too many mistakes in your life to ever be happy? That life is too difficult to get right? That you couldn't possibly turn around all your wrongs? I have most definitely felt this way. *To Hell With You* is a story of a young girl, me, who set out to find the answers to the age-old questions of: Why are we here? What is our purpose? What the young me found was nothing but broken dreams and heartache. Yet beneath the pain, upon peering under the mistakes, were some answers to these questions. Come with me! But know that you are about to embark upon a rollercoaster of an adventure. I hope that you feel everything! Descend with me into the dark, ugly, raw, not-so-pretty parts of my story into the triumphs of perseverance and hope that unfold into discovery.

I must also tell you that I have been hesitant to share my story. I have wrestled during the twenty years that I have been working on this book, that you might think that I am weak and therefore, my story is not worth reading. To my doubt, I admit that my behavior was less than perfect and some choices may seem to have been extreme. But, on the other hand, to convey what I uncovered without descending into hell, well, there would be no credence to my words if all I shared were the victories and left out my imperfect humanity. Honestly, I don't know how else to be.

We are a society failing in our internal, emotional capacity to understand the process of supposed failure, of unrealized hopes and expectations. If we are to thrive not just survive, we need to change how we approach life and unlearn what we have been taught, to understand life differently.

I have come to realize that to be vulnerable is a strength in being human. Exposing my humanity here is a way for you to come with me to discover the beauty within the vulnerability. It's not comfortable, I know. If you get to a point where you are repelled by the book and want to throw it against the wall, do it! But go back later, pick it up and finish it. Do not leave yourself in the valley of despair, disgust, frustration, or whatever negative emotion you find yourself in. You must get out of the valley with me to reach the top of the mountain. Then, if you still feel the same, throw it again, against the wall and leave it there.

If my title offends you, it is not meant to. The title is a double entendre, it has two meanings. As you read and contemplate my story, I think you will be able to decipher the meanings and why this book could go by no other name.

And frankly, I am an idealist. I do believe we all are good; we all want to live in a good world, and we all want to have a good life. And although I forsook my ideals for a time, I can't live without them. They push me forward to not quit. There were periods when I felt that it was far too difficult to change the trajectory of my life, death seemed easier. Had I continued to believe that, I would not have been able to raise my four boys, my life would not have changed and this story would not have come to print.

This is our story. It is true, and these things did happen. Two of us set out on a journey, soon we became three and then four. One of us did not come back. This book is written from my best recollection of the events and discussions that happened and is, therefore, a transparent account. Nevertheless, this story does not define me, or the people involved. That's the funny thing, or more like the ironic thing about life. Our stories don't define us. We choose to define ourselves, consciously or unconsciously, from the stories we perpetuate within. Life's difficulties give us tools, if we can perceive them, then we can use them to define ourselves. My boys and I have taken some of these diamonds that have been forged from the fire of our hell to realize that we alone create our lives; the responsibility is ours and the journey never ends.

I am blessed to be the mother of four beautiful young men. It has been my most difficult responsibility while simultaneously my greatest honor and joy. I am a teacher. I also am a sound bath practitioner and an energy worker. I have a BA from the University of Southern California in Los Angeles and MA from the Universidad de Salamanca in Spain. But all credentials aside, and most importantly, I survived. I am proof that we can pick ourselves up after a great fall to bless our neighbor, to believe in the good in us all and to hope again. I am an example, not to perfection, mind you, and not without scars and certainly not with all the answers. But an example of the human will, not just to survive, but thrive.

The book is divided into four sections. Part one introduces you to the main people in this story, the background and the 'why' of the choices made. Part two is our journey. Part three is the aftermath and how we picked up the pieces of an indescribable loss. And finally, part four delves into the diamonds forged from the fire of hell.

When you finish reading this book, you will have felt every possible emotion. It is an adventure filled with a multitude of emotions from anger, disappointment, elation, fear, sadness, frustration, joy, anticipation, disgust, hope, inspiration and more. You will know that anyone can go through great defeat and resist becoming jaded. In addition, I share mindsets embedded with tools that thwart off the patterns of resentment that build in our minds that if left unchecked, will create a life we do not recognize nor like. I have used these mindsets in my life and I believe you may relate to them and may apply them on your own journey as well. These mindsets will help you to:

* Process the patterns of pain
* Find a different understanding of forgiveness
* Trade the trauma of failure for freedom
* Grasp gratitude in light of grief
* Learn that love is the foundation of all life

"Is it a bad idea to share my story?" I asked my youngest son. "I mean, what if people think I am weak? Or they criticize and say, 'Well, I'd never do that!'?"

"Mom, no. You're not weak!" He said with tenderness. "If people think that, then they missed the whole point of the book. How can anyone be strong if they haven't been weak?"

PART I

Hell

Trip threw open the door from the back bedroom. He made his way down the hallway, stumbling over nothing, bracing himself on the walls. Terror filled his eyes.

"I can't stay here anymore! I have to go or God is going to kill me! I broke my vow when I married you! The scripture warns to be careful not to break your vows to men, much less God," He rambled.

My hands went moist. My body began to tremble, but I couldn't move. The black abyss of fear gripped me like nightfall overtaking a summer sunset. I was afraid for the first time in our six-year marriage.

Trip paced the floor, up and back and back and forth. He ran his hands through his thick, black hair, frantically seeking the nearest exit. Eyes that once suggested calm, Mediterranean waters were now raging seas.

"I have never been free from guilt for marrying you. I think God is holding me accountable. I have to nullify the marriage."

My eyes fluttered. I put my hand up as if telling him to stop. "What!? Wait! What vow!? When!?"

Shaking my head no, I said in disbelief. "You've never spoken of this before! Why?" My hands on my head now. "What are you saying? "Is this an excuse for you? A way out?"

Trip didn't even hear my questions nor did he feel my incredulity. "Maybe God will spare me." He cowered before me, then, like the strike of a snake, he came at me. "You aren't safe either. Remember we left our families because of the admonition in the New Testament." I recoiled.

⌇

Deep within my soul—the space where courage and strength lie—is a familiar place. I have had to visit there often. It is that place where I find the will and strength to confront life's trials. I went there again. I knew the inventory well, and my stores were wearing thin. I knew that when the supply ran out, I would die. Without hesitation, I gathered the fragments of will that remained in order to calm my husband. My commitment to him compelled me to try.

"Trip, ss-sit down. L-let me make you some tea." I stuttered. "Chamomile. I-it should calm your nerves."

Trip sat at our makeshift table; the one he made from a display case we bought at a drug store going out of business. He sat in an oversized office chair we'd lugged around from place to place. It was here he ate, read, and studied the scripture. It was the last night he would ever sit in that chair.

I walked to the stove and prepared his tea. I closed my eyes and took a long, deep breath. Then, I turned to bring him a steaming mug. I sat opposite him on a wooden dining chair. We looked at each other across the table.

"Cubby, I'm scared," he said.

Cubby was his nickname for me. He likened us to two cub

bears, playfully being together. There was a time that it seemed that we were that way.

"I don't know what to do? I want to jump out of my skin. I'm going to burn!".

I shuddered and swallowed hard. My voice quavered as I said, "Trip, you, you're going to be alright. God is forgiving. He knows we make mistakes." My eyes reached for him, pleading for him to come back to me from his darkness. "I know it is difficult, but look outside yourself. Think about the boys. Think about us. Don't you think God would rather you take responsibility for having a family and forget your promise of the past? We, our family, replace that vow now." I took another breath. "He has pardoned you for the sake of the ones you have involved. God is good." He didn't say anything, he just seemed to listen.

We used to sit and talk for hours like a couple at a café sharing the inner thoughts of an intimate relationship. It was nice. Through the years, though, we talked less and less and he talked more and more, but this time he yearned for my thoughts. I liked it. I had hoped our marriage would have contained more of these moments. In that moment, Trip reminded me of the consideration, and care he used to show me.

I remembered a similar incident when our son, Kuder, was about a year old. Again, he came out of the room. This time with a bounce in his step, grinning. He was excited, like he had good tickets to see his favorite sports team and he was on his way.

"Let's go out to eat," he said, motioning toward the door.

That night he took us to a nice restaurant, helped me off with my coat, and pulled out my chair. We talked about the future. He smiled as he spoke and sometimes we laughed. He even played with Kuder. Every once in a while, he would reach over and touch my hand. And then, from out of nowhere, he said, "You're beautiful! You're a good wife and mother." He paused. "Any man would be lucky to have you."

For an instant, I was taken aback. It had been a long time since he talked to me in this way.

Smiling he continued, "I have found a pearl of great price."

My heart was wrenched with emotion. He loved me! And I adored him. I looked down at my arms now crossed over one another hugging my waist. My eyes filled with tears. I bounced from the chair and jumped into his lap. Half laughing, half crying, I incessantly kissed his face.

The thought of that tender moment, from what seemed so long ago, brought me back to our makeshift table. His countenance was soft, just like on that night, long ago. The cool pools of water were soothing to look at again. He reached for me and took my wrist. He held it tight, rubbing his thumb on the top side of my hand as if he had something desperate to say to me. Only silence fell. We looked into each other's eyes, and I could swear that a hint of mist clouded the pools of water.

"Thank you for the tea," he managed.

"You're welcome," I whispered.

Thank God! We're going to come out of this, I thought. Hope grew in my belly; thankful I had given him the remaining fragments of my being. I had nothing more to give.

He looked down at our hands laced together then touched them with his other hand. Staring at them, he gradually let go. He rose from the table and turned away from me. His head tilted down, gazing at the floor, hands in his pockets. He seemed to be moving something with this foot as if in deep thought. He started to turn back around to me. I anticipated open arms, but as he turned, I was horrified. The caged lion had returned. The violent seas in his eyes could no longer be contained. He looked about wildly, with nowhere to run.

"I have to go. I can't stay here," he said as he pushed by me toward the door and I stumbled to run to Kuder playing in the living room in case Trip had any thoughts of harming him or taking Kuder with him. I put my trembling arms around him with my body as a shield. My stomach churned in knots.

Throughout our marriage I could always find some path to rationalize his actions, but he was drifting further away, down a path I did not understand. A path I could not follow.

Not anymore.

Spain

Ten years earlier

The winter chill of January welcomed us as we landed in Paris. The humidity seeped through my clothes—a sharp reminder I was no longer in the temperate climate of Southern California. Europe was experiencing record-cold temperatures that year. Even so, my blood boiled with excitement. My childhood dream of studying abroad was materializing. It was my freshman year at the University of Southern California (USC).

One hundred USC students studied abroad that spring. Most of us were from the United States, with the largest concentration of students from the West Coast and others from the Midwest, East, and South, and a few foreign students, as well. We were strangers when our trip began, unaware that our experiences would in some small way bond us together. Paris was our first stop.

Notre Dame was the first of many ancient cathedrals we would visit. Never having entered an ancient cathedral before, I hoped to find spiritual warmth within her walls. Back home, church seemed dead to me. It was either old people who occupied the pews, hoping to find absolution for their lives or women looking for the companionship they lacked from their husbands. And there were those who flocked to the aegis of the church to find solace due to tragedy. I longed for people my age who sought a greater spiritual purpose rather than just fire insurance from hell.

There she stood, Notre Dame; two impressive towers protecting the central medallion of glass, reflecting hues of blue and violet. Three arched entrances beckoned us to enter. Prompted by our guide, we stepped over the threshold into the nave of an enormous interior. Pillars, thick enough to hide a small car, stood like soldiers guarding her heart that rose to apex into gothic arches.

Everything was gray: the walls, the pillars, the arches; it was cold, with no life, no warmth. Her only color was the stained glass, which was not enough to conceal her void.

I fixated on the altar: the familiar monument of the slain Jesus displayed for all to see, the trademark of all Catholic churches. In an instant, I was five years old again, staring at Jesus nailed to the cross and feeling a warm light in my chest. I knelt on the hassock and put my hands together for prayer. My arms could barely rest on the pew in front of me. I respectfully made the sign of the cross. The lace from my veil made the statues of the risen Jesus, the Holy Mother and the Saints, hazy. Candles glimmered, casting shadows on their faces, as if they were alive. They frightened me, but Amá, as my brothers and sister called my mother, said the house of God was safe so I had nothing to fear. I turned my head from statue to statue to see if I could catch one move.

"*Estáte quieta! Estamos en la casa de Dios!*"

"Be still! We are in the house of God!" Amá scolded as I felt her thumb and forefinger grab flesh from my upper arm and twist. How I hated when she did that! I bowed my head in shame, angered that she had the power to make me do her will, knowing that if I didn't I would be in big trouble. All I wanted was to see Jesus move. Amá said He was God and that God lived. I hoped to sit with Him like children sat with Santa Claus.

My mother grew up Catholic with great faith in the church. My father was Catholic as well, but he didn't put much faith in the clergy. He believed religion was more for convenience's sake than spirituality. He often excused himself from the Sunday rituals for serenity in nature. Both parents stressed love, hard work, and honor, but my mother placed these beliefs in the context of religion, while my father offered that the world ran on certain laws of nature. My father never stressed his beliefs, and knowingly said, "Children follow the beliefs of their mother," and he was good with that.

My parents emigrated from Mexico and settled in the foothills of the Sierra in Northern California in the 1950s. It was a time when just a few immigrant families lived in the Gold Country; a time when education placed those who spoke other languages in classes for students with special needs. We began as outcasts, and therefore developed strong bonds, defending each other from the onslaughts of peers and the society we now lived in, until we gained respect in our community. I am the sixth of seven children: five brothers, my older sister, and me.

We carried different yokes, the women and men in my family. The responsibility of serving the men fell on the women. My brothers never made a meal, straightened their rooms, or cleaned the bathrooms. My sister and I were expected to do these tasks, following my mother's example. The boys, on the other hand, were our custodians of safety and worked outside with Dad.

Once I snuck outside to help stack the firewood. Dad caught me and instead of scolding me for abandoning my mother, he reprimanded my brother. "How come you let your sister carry the firewood?" It was Dad's command that the boys watch out for the women in the family. If any harm came to us on one of my brother's watches, there would be hell to pay. No harm ever came.

As we entered our teens, my sister and I noticed that our American sisters had different responsibilities than ours. They easily played sports like my brothers, easily had boyfriends, and got to go out without having to jump through, what felt like a million hoops before leaving the house. They didn't have to clean up after everyone. My brothers' yoke seemed better than the yoke carried by my sister and me. Sometimes it felt like we were more like the slaves doing the menial jobs while the boys got the glory. Soon, my sister began to protest our traditions. Although for the most part I joined her on her quest for freedom, a part of me found pleasure and satisfaction in serving my brothers and Dad. Their gratitude was evident in their eyes, and I never felt taken for granted. At a moment's notice, I could count on them for anything, like help with fixing something, painting my room, getting rid of a big potato bug stuffed between my dresser and the wall, or even kicking someone's ass if I was troubled. I thought this to be a fair trade. We had different burdens to bear.

I began to shiver and realized I was freezing as the cross came back into focus. I was no longer a young girl, no longer with my family in Northern California, but realizing a childhood dream in Europe.

The rest of my group had left the altar and now stood at the far end of the cathedral listening to our guide. I quickly caught up with them as we continued into a maze of small chapels.

Statues of saints stood like gravestones in a forgotten cemetery, long since dead, yet something whispered that the church contained secrets; secrets I could not yet hear. I cinched my coat to keep from shivering. I had to get out, both cold and disappointed that the warmth I eagerly anticipated was not housed here.

I walked out of the frigid cathedral into the sunlight. I welcomed the contrast and anticipated finding warmth; instead the sun did little to alleviate the pins and needles poking my flesh. I shuddered, unsure if it was from the cathedral standing centuries without heat or from the haunting of spiritual death.

Our brief introduction to France was ending, but not before taking a quick peek down Avenue-des Champs-Élysées and up the Eiffel Tower, an evening boat ride down the Seine River and a visit to the Louvre.

The Mona Lisa, the famed lady with a faint smile, was the attraction we all wanted to see. Most of us hurried to the floor where she rests beneath a box of what looked like glass. She was locked up. I couldn't get close enough to contemplate her in silence. People huddled around her almost constantly. I observed her at a distance. She looked trapped, in a box. It bothered me.

Madrid, like Paris, met us with bitter cold. We had little time to notice, for the moment we arrived, our semester began with an excursion to Northern Spain. Our history class never met in a classroom. Instead, classes were held all over the country. In these classrooms, we poked our fingers into the mouths of gaping gargoyles, ran our hands along rough arches of a Roman aqueduct, heard voices of classmates travel through the Alhambra, shared a drink with a Spaniard in the Plaza Mayor, danced Flamenco with Sevillanas, felt the political unrest as Valencianos set fire to their floats, breathed in the lost fragrance of ancient gardens, tasted the simply-spiced food, and contemplated the painted eyes of El Greco peering back at us.

Our excursions took us out of Madrid for weekends at a time, affording us time to become more familiar with each other. Fifteen of us visited a discotheque one night after a day of walking on uneven cobblestone streets, viewing the countryside from atop fortified walls and entering yet another ancient cathedral.

We approached the discothèque and pressed through a crowd of eager attendees. Dark paint hiding red damask walls raised a few stories in a sphere. I peered through the smoky air. Slowly taking shape through the haze were darkened box seats and vacant candelabras. Disfigured nymphs, now used as hardware for hanging colored lighting and sound equipment, hinted to a forgotten time. Recycled theater seats and partially lit chandeliers whispered that ballets, concerts, and plays once echoed within these walls. Now liquor, cigarettes, and contemporary music were its main attractions.

We danced for hours. "Born in the USA" by Bruce Springsteen played when I finally took a break. I rested in an empty theater seat and watched my classmates enjoy themselves to the sounds of The Boss. My eyes were drawn to Mary, dancing with the others while holding a drink in her hand.

Alcohol spilled on the wooden floor as she danced, singing with pride that she was born in the USA. Her thin bleached-blond hair caught drifts of air as she stumbled. Her tan skin and crow's feet fanning out from the corners of her eyes when she smiled, revealed an older woman, even though though she was young. She was playing the social game, yet her eyes said she wanted something more; not just to be the typical obnoxious college kid in Europe. Was Mary like me? Were her insecurity and vulnerability mine? Maybe she and I shared the same searching heart. I longed for something more and hoped my typical behavior would render authenticity.

Enticed by the lively Spanish nightlife, we stayed out until the early hours of dawn. Our wake-up call seemed to come earlier than usual the next morning. We dragged our feet onto the plush tour bus eager to sink into a seat and curl up with a Walkman. We stopped at a twelfth century castle on our way back into Madrid. As our professor unfolded his lecture from the east tower, I envisioned the queen addressing her loyal subjects in the courtyard below centuries before I would come to stand in that very place.

Each night, I went to sleep thanking God I was there, and each morning I awoke with the anticipation of a new experience. Despite my good fortune, I could not suppress my desire for something more. I wanted to know the purpose of life. As I walked the streets of adventure, emptiness never failed to show its shadow behind a distant pillar or in a vacant seat at the bar.

We visited El Monasterio de Piedra in the latter part of our history course. Nine centuries before, the present-day hotel was a monastery whose monks created a paradise out of the existing landscape. Every tree, boulder, and vine appeared to have been purposely placed to awaken man's spirituality. Even the waterfalls that fell into streams bending through wildflower-filled meadows elicited thoughts of a deeper purpose. My classmates Don, Kurt, and I agreed we'd return to this place and experience its magic again before returning to the States.

I first met Don on our seventeen-hour flight leaving Los Angeles, over the US and then the Atlantic to land in Paris. During one of the changes of musical chairs in our confined quarters, he sat by me. I welcomed his sincere blue eyes framed by layered blond hair. He asked if I wanted to listen to his Walkman. I agreed and heard Christian music. It soothed me amidst the insecurity of leaving the security I had known. It was my first year in college, my first year living on my own in Los Angeles, and now my first visit to Europe. Through him, I met Kurt, one of the baton leaders in the USC marching band. They befriended me, persuading me to come to their religious gatherings, but I kept them at arm's distance. I didn't want my voyage in Europe to be disturbed by some guilt trip that their pious behavior elicited. They reminded me of my mother saying, *"que diria dios?"* "What would God say?"

I wanted to explore! I liked their company though, and they proved to be my closest companions that semester, even though they were Protestants and I was Catholic.

Time in Spain swelled with the overload of all things new, yet the inevitable happened: the semester came to an end. Finals were taken, books returned, and goodbyes said.

The questions to my purpose in life clouded my future path. I felt I couldn't go on until I had some answers. Don, Kurt, one of Don's friends named Jezzi, who was traveling through Europe at that time and I, all of us, did return to the monastery. And it was here, at this historically sacred place that I embraced Christianity and found people my age who sought a greater spiritual purpose. Finally, the direction for my life became clear. Or so I thought.

Love

Nestled in the forest of Northern California, up Highway 50, sat the Pony Express Inn. The pines, like soldiers, stood at attention guarding their post. Smoke emanated from the chimney contrasting the night sky, heavy at first then dissipating into the stars. It was a small, rustic place known for its great steaks and warm atmosphere. Hand in hand, Trip and I walked up the wooden steps onto the porch.

"Wait here a moment while I check if our table is ready," he said.

He gave my hand a reassuring squeeze then excused himself inside. I turned to look up at the stars and took a long, deep breath. The scent of smoldering oak mixed with the fragrance of pine after a December rain lingered in the air. The crisp night aroma nourished my body as I savored the taste.

I pondered the conversation that introduced me to Trip as I waited on the porch. I returned from Spain no longer Catholic and now a part of Faith Community Church in Southern California—a large non-denominational church with 10,000 members.

"Hey, did you girls hear about Trip's version of true love?" Jezzi asked as she teasingly rubbed her shoulder up to mine. The girls in the college department all thought Trip was a deeply spiritual man. He always seemed to impress us with his insight.

"No, what? Do tell," The girls clamored as we all scrunched together.

"Well," Jezzi continued, "according to Trip, true love would manifest itself in the most vulnerable of situations; like, say vomiting in the bathroom."

"Eww!" one girl exclaimed.

"Yeah, I know," Jezzie concurred. "But let me finish. So, okay, while you threw up your last remnants of dignity, your true love would hold you tight, then clean your face, lovingly dabbing it with a cloth," Jezzi concluded while she playfully dabbed my face. We all giggled visualizing the scenario.

"Well! I'd rather suffer alone," one girl said.

"Yeah, I have my dignity to uphold," another said.

"That might be cute, but I think it's disgusting!" Jezzi added.

I said nothing, but I was intrigued. Trip had bypassed the superficial in a relationship. This was how I wanted to be loved.

I caught myself grinning as Trip returned, reciprocating my smile. All was set.

Our eyes met a fire glowing on the opposite side of the inn. Old West antiques adorned the walls and vacant corners of the restaurant.

A young man dressed like a bartender out of the Old West greeted us and then ushered us to a secluded table. Illuminated by table candles and wall sconces, that small corner of the restaurant became our enchanted world for the evening.

I relished the thought of how lucky I felt to be with the man I adored. I remembered playing under the magnolia tree in our front yard when I was a little girl. In my mind's eye flashed a picture of a man. He had black hair conservatively cut, contrasting his cream complexion on which he wore Clark Kent glasses; the same eyeglasses Trip wore when he studied.

Trip was everything I dreamed he would be. He stood on pillars of muscular legs that broadened to protective shoulders, shielding me like a sturdy oak. He drew out my femininity under the shelter of his manliness. I loved how he made me feel: delicate and dainty. His eyes were like the crystal sea of blue waters; deep and dimensional.

We barely spoke. Only momentarily did we take our eyes off each other. As we methodically ate our dinners, I allowed myself to be completely consumed in his gaze. The intensity of his stare almost felt like his hands were caressing my body, taking inventory of my every curve. Under this man's unrelenting gaze, I had become malleable clay in his presence. He could have become a master potter, but not that night. Even though every natural impulse in my body was saying, "Take me!"

He cleaned his plate. I only picked at mine. He released my hand and then reached for something under the table while he slid off the chair onto one knee. From his uncurled hand, he produced a little black box. Stunned, I couldn't take my eyes off it. *Is this what I think it is? No, it's too soon.* I argued with myself. I had known Trip for two years now, but we'd only been dating for three months. I managed to look up at him. He was watching me with a knowing smile, savoring my every move. As if in slow motion, he opened the box. My eyes widened as he opened the small container. I was speechless. My eyes focused on the glimmer in the center of the box. It was beautiful, shining like a thousand brilliant stars. On either side of the ring formed two pyramids of baguettes, five on each side. Elevated between the baguette pyramids sat a one-carat, princess-cut diamond. His deep voice broke the silence.

"I chose this setting because it looks like a crown. It's fit for a queen. You are my queen." He looked down at the box.

I still couldn't move.

"I want you to marry me," he said.

I gasped, grabbing my face with my hands. I wanted nothing more than to marry this man, to unselfishly give of myself out of the pure, raw emotion of love, nothing less. I thought it insincere to give to a partner merely because of a marriage agreement. I wanted love to compel me. I knew love came when it pleased, but I had hoped I would find that inexplicable force that draws you to a person who makes your soul sing. A love that sees the good despite their imperfections and where you will do the unthinkable for this person for which people deem you crazy, but you know you are not. You simply love them. I believed in this love, and it had come to me. Every nerve in my body hummed. I was alive.

He gently took my hands from my face and brought me to my feet. "Hey, are you with me?" he asked.

I caught myself both trembling and tearing up in delight. I couldn't believe that this amazing man had just proposed. I said yes and melted into his masculine-scented chest, wrapped in his wanting arms. Our lips were drawn together, like metal drawn to magnets. I knew he wanted me, even though I sensed an intangible emptiness in his closeness. I didn't heed the vague revelation. Nothing could have penetrated my dream.

Us

E vening settled on our 1940's home. Trip sat in a white, Queen Anne chair, pouring over his Bible. I reclined, smiling at the debonair man who sat opposite me. Through the Victorian glass lamp, I contemplated him. We didn't own a television set. The media has a way of superimposing societal norms on unsuspecting viewers. We wanted to come to our own conclusions. So I watched my husband. Trip reminded me of Gregory Peck in— *To Kill a Mockingbird*, sitting in his chair reading his book; handsome and stately with his jet black hair and reading glasses. He dreamed of being a pastor; sharing the information he learned from his studies. I didn't think it was a good idea since he himself doubted his salvation. "How can you lead others when you yourself don't know the way?" His shoulders slumped forward followed by his head as he nodded in regretful agreement.

"Cubby, Cubby," Trip repeated.

"Oh, yes, what is it?" I replied, coming back into the moment.

"I think I got something here. I've been thinking about this since your little brother came over the other day." He quoted from the Book of Matthew: 'He that loves father and mother more than me is not worthy of me . . . and he that loses his life for my sake shall find it.'

He flipped to another verse in the New Testament. 'Sell your possessions and give alms and then you will have treasure in heaven.'

"You know we've been questioning true salvation," he said, excitement brewing.

"Yeah."

"How Christians claim to possess the power of God, but are no different than anyone else?"

I nodded.

"Maybe we've been going about salvation all wrong. Maybe we have to do something radically different. What if the reason we're not seeing the truth is because we need to do these things first?"

"What things? What are you saying?" I asked

"I think we need to sell our possessions and leave our families."

I heard an enormous crack in the earth. My ears roared. My head spun. If Trip had said anything after these words I didn't hear. A painful pit of darkness nailed me in the gut. I felt instantly weak and simultaneously trapped, but I had to move. I rose from the couch and reached for anything to brace myself. The only thing available was the lamp. It, too, stumbled and nearly fell with the weight of my grasp. I needed air. I was holding my breath. I had to get outside. There was no air to breathe in the house.

"I, I'm going for a walk." I stuttered as I walked out the door.

Trip seemed unconcerned as he nodded and returned to his reading.

A few days earlier, my little brother had come to visit with some news. He too had become a Christian while in college.

"Guys, I'm gonna drop out of school," he proclaimed.

"What? You have one more year," I said.

"I'm a sojourner in this world waiting for my life to begin after death. What I do now is not important."

Trip was inspired and the two of them talked until late that evening. My little brother showed intestinal fortitude that Trip admired. But I never thought my brother's choice would push Trip to these conclusions. I wanted solid answers, too. I wanted that which is honorable, enduring and profoundly inherent in all of us, but my family?

We'd only been married a year and already I faced a crossroads. Either my husband was wrong and our marriage was over, or he was right and I would have to leave my family.

It was August in the foothills of Northern California. The evening breeze felt good against my skin. Even so, a shiver ran down my spine thinking of Trip's words. I rubbed my hands up and down my arms. My mind raced.

We couldn't get around the fact that after the initial elation of salvation we had begun to fall back into our old ways. What we once fervently preached became dull among the everyday duties of life. We wondered how this could be if a supernatural power was at work.

The church explained that the soul is dead, housed within an imperfect body. Upon conversion, our soul becomes new but is still the adversary to our physical bodies. Once more, society is at odds with our soul. Our quest then was to utilize the power of salvation to overcome personal and worldly struggles.

We observed moral people wrestling with personal and worldly struggles, as well. The question remained that if

Christians were given a power greater than non-Christians, surely the souls' desires would prevail, otherwise, we would have to conclude that we were no different than anyone else. But how could this be?

I made my way through the oak and pine-covered hills.

What was I going to do? The weight of half the earth crushed my heart. I never dreamed our discussions would lead to this crossroads. How could I leave my family? How could he ask this of me?

I cleared my head and considered a divorce.

But what if he is right?

Two summers before, I had served on a mission in New York City. Twelve of us went to a park to "share the gospel" to homeless people. One afternoon, a couple of tough-looking men attempted to come on to one of us girls.

Jezzie, the same friend of Don whom I had met in Spain, methodically and without letting anyone detect what she was doing. (But I saw her!) She had removed herself from the group to a spot where she could be prominently noticed by one of the homeless men. Her plan worked. One man saw she had placed herself apart from the cluster of protection and began to holler obscene advances at her. Putting on an air of naiveté, she began to talk back to the man, while feigning tears of violation as he continued talking crudely to her. In an instant, she was encircled by our boys coming to her rescue, telling the crass violator to leave her alone.

I stood apart from the group in utter disbelief. I couldn't believe what I was witnessing! The boys questioned incessantly, "Are you alright? Poor Jezzie! That must have been horrible to have such a man speak to you in that way!" Curiously, the Christian boys left the rest of us girls unprotected.

We left the park to meet the rest of our group across town. In complete credulity, everyone was retelling Jezzie's horrible encounter. Even the leaders came to comfort her. They gave her hugs and words of support. With big beautiful teary eyes, she gulped the attention. The boys, from then on, took particular care to watch out for her.

I was stunned! I saw the deception unfold before my eyes as if I was watching a movie. Jezzie was my friend.

I knew this sort of manipulation happened in the 'world', but Christians proclaimed the power of God had changed them to leave those games behind. If Christians are compelled by truth, how could she do this? It was obvious that she wanted attention, to have everyone come to her aid, but she deceived those around her to attain it.

I began to lose faith on that trip. Something wasn't right. Could it be that Christians flock under the wings of the church to claim strength from God only to run from their shortcomings exposed by society? Is it that Christians can't make it in the 'world' so they seek an easier sub-society to dominate? I didn't leave the world; it just went by a different name.

Maybe Trip's solution was right. Maybe it was the only way to find an authentic path. Power, I knew, existed in truth. Great and beautiful things could happen if mankind could grab hold of the spiritual forces that flow around us. Only this path seemed to elude us. Truth had to exist, and I was compelled to find it.

It was dark now and I found myself back at our front door. I staggered into the house and found Trip at the dining room table studying. I knew from his excitement he had already made his decision. He opened his mouth, "If we don't have truth, then we are not saved, which means we are still going to hell along with everyone in the church, not to mention those outside the church."

He paused. "Could we have uncovered a truth covered by lies? Cubby, we have to save ourselves. Heaven and hell are in the balance."

The consequence made the choice clear.

"I think you're right," I managed.

The moment I concurred, the understanding of what I was about to do became real and flooded my heart with a tidal wave of anguish.

Goodbye

Mom came to visit the next day. I was washing the dishes when I heard a knock at the door. Trip stood at the front door before I had a chance to dry my hands. I saw my mother, through the windows on the front porch, carrying a basket of fruit from her garden to share. The cast of indoor shadows hid me from her view. She expected to be invited in, but Trip would not let her pass.

"We have decided to leave the family and from this moment on we will not speak to you or your children." Trip's face was dark and solemn. Why did he have to speak so harshly to my mother?

Still at the kitchen sink, I bowed my head unable to move. He quoted to her the scriptures of the night before showing what led to our decision and explained that the severance was necessary to find the truth. I managed to lift my head and caught a glimpse of my mother struggling; as though she were watching her child drown, powerless to stop it. I sank to my knees. My heart swelled, ready to explode. This is not how I wanted to say goodbye. I felt a violent shove to carry out the separation.

I learned later that she ran home to tell the rest of the family in hopes that someone could stop this nightmare, but there was nothing anyone could have done.

I said goodbye to my firefighter brother first. I never did say goodbye to my other brothers who lived in different parts of the state. My sister, who did live nearby, thought this whole thing was ridiculous and not worth discussing.

I thought if anyone might understand, it was him. He knew my heart better than anyone. Also, when I was gone, my parents would need someone to ask over and over, "Why?"

I went alone to the California Department of Forestry and Fire Protection station across town as Trip packed, dreading the conversation I was to have. My third oldest brother was a fireman stationed there that summer. He stood at the doorway knowing the purpose of my visit, yet he wore a warm smile. We hugged. His closeness begged me not to go. A flood of tender memories flipped through my mind.

Homecoming my senior year in high school bustled with half-time festivities. The other candidates asked boyfriends to escort them. I chose my brother to do the honors. He came from Southern California that night, despite the fact that he was a starving college student. He arrived just minutes before the ceremony, handsomely dressed in a black suit and tie. As we stood together, I sensed his pride. I knew nothing could have kept him from being there.

"Wave to your peasant friends," he joked as the cameras flashed.

He led me to the convertible waiting to take me around the football field. He kissed my cheek, patted the car and said, "Have fun." And as suddenly as he arrived he was gone.

I was brought back to the present when my brother said, "Take care of the baby."

Our eyes locked. I hesitated. *How did he know I was pregnant? I had found out myself only a few days ago.* I said nothing then sheepishly smiled and turned to walk away, his hands still lingering on my waist.

I drove away, watching him through the rearview mirror. Our eyes embraced until broken by a turn in the road. As the road straightened, I slumped over as if I had been shot. I wondered if I would lose my first child; the pain in my belly seemed too hostile an environment to sustain a new life. I looked back. Again, he was gone, but this time forever I thought for sure.

The pain magnified when Trip and I drove to make the last visit to my parent's home, the only home I had ever known. I had to tell my parents that leaving was my decision, too. I got out of the sedan. Trip remained outside leaning against the car, his arms folded. I placed my foot on the sidewalk and started down the path leading to my parents who waited for me on the front porch. I felt like the condemned walking the plank. How I wished I was that little girl again, running up the sidewalk to throw myself into my mother's arms after a day at school.

Our eyes met and I saw a tinge of forgiveness already in hers. She stood alongside Dad. I fumbled for words. I turned to look at Dad, his eyes vacant, glossy with unshed tears. He was not a man of many words.

I remembered when I was a teenager and Jimmy had called to ask me out again.

I had asked Dad a billion times if I could go with him, but he would not answer. After what seemed like an eternity, he responded,

"Mi'ja, a man wants to be kept guessing. If every time he asks you to go somewhere and you say yes, then he will expect your willingness. Never let him feel he completely has you. In this way, he will cherish you and work to win your love."

My answer was 'no' when Jimmy called back.

And just as my father had predicted, every date Jimmy planned afterward was different, given more thought.

The wisdom of my father would not be fully understood until years later.

Now, I found myself face-to-face with my Dad as he fought to understand my thinking. I wanted to tell my parents I loved them, but those words meant nothing in light of my actions.

I smiled tenderly. My parents responded in kind. I reached and touched my mothers hand and then my father's arm, one arm out to each. I couldn't find the words to say anything. Nor could they. Our eyes met. There was love, concern and incomprehensibility in theirs. I held back my tears. I don't know how I did. I knew if I started to cry, the torrent could not be contained and it would only serve to deter me from what I had to do. Inside my bowels tumbled like a commercial dryer, such internal pain. I was letting go of the very family who had given me the strength to leave it.

Trip and I left my parents' house. As we drove past the high school, I couldn't go any further. I asked him to pull over, pushed out of the car, and ran to the steps where I stumbled to sit. My tears gushed with unimaginable sorrow. How do you say good-bye when death is not the reaper?

I traded my family for a hope-a hope that I would find the truth; truth the Church claimed to possess, but I could not see it.

Despite my tumult, I parted with my family never to be rid of a sorrow that would become my constant companion.

Goodbye Again

Thaddeus Nero Danovich III was named after his father, who was named after his father. Trip, for short.

I understood Trip's grandfather. Like me, he was a first-generation child of immigrant parents, attended USC, and had many brothers and sisters. He and his wife started a family grocery store in Southern California, working long hours to make a good life for themselves.

Trip's father also attended USC, where he met Trip's mother, but he confused me. He was a white male who made his fortune in the Silicon Valley. He seemed uneasy with me, too. Maybe because I am Mexican and my family didn't have money. Maybe because he was uncomfortable with his own son and therefore me, or maybe it was simply my insecurity that drew us apart.

My Trip was a hard worker. He taught himself Greek and Hebrew. He became an All-American soccer player and attended Stanford University on a full scholarship, where he majored in electrical engineering. Trip was spiritual, smart, refined, and athletic. He was my man.

"We came here to tell you that we will be leaving the family," Trip said, forcing his shoulders back, feigning confidence. "We believe the Bible is telling us to sell our possessions and leave our families."

"You're not going to sell our family heirlooms, are you?" Trip's mom interrupted. "Those antiques must remain in the family. The rest you can do with whatever you wish," she stipulated.

Trip agreed, then continued his sermon, but his father stopped him saying, "Trip, I don't need to hear anymore." He took a puff of his cigar and slowly exhaled. The white smoke framed his confident countenance. "Do what you must, but realize your inheritance will be split among your other brothers."

"What about my trust from Aunt Kate?" Trip asked.

"That money has already been divided. I am referring to any funds disbursed hereafter from your mother and me," he clarified.

I watched from one of the posh couches Trip's mother had refurbished every time she changed her décor. *Why wasn't he speaking as harshly to his parents as he had to my mother?*

"I don't understand why you have to do this, Trip," his mother said, dabbing her tears.

"So, what? We'll never see you again?" Trip's youngest brother asked.

"Yeah," Trip confirmed.

"Whatever; if that makes you happy," his brother said, leaving the room.

I met Trip when he was in his late twenties, and by that time he either didn't want to follow in his father's footsteps, or couldn't. Their relationship already had a pattern of tension. He was the oldest of four boys, and his father expected him to carry on the family legacy—the first born son is to be more successful than his father before him. But after two unsuccessful attempts to make the German and US soccer teams and a failed father-son working relationship, I think his father gave up on Trip.

PART II

Leaving

The crayon yellow moving van drew attention to itself on the curb, packed and ready to go. Trip hastened us to be on our way. I welcomed the idea. I didn't want to endure the pain of another goodbye. We only lacked a suitcase to pack our clothes. We had always borrowed luggage from my family, thinking we would eventually get a set we liked. That time never came.

We went to Kmart for a quick and cheap purchase. Trip grabbed the biggest case he could find and we made our way to the checkout counter.

I walked down the aisle in front of him when my childhood friend Monique came around the corner. We had grown up together and her family lived just down the road from us. Monique had honey-colored hair and eyes. She wore her hair short around her delicate features atop an equally petite frame.

We greeted each other and she graciously asked about my mother and father. I hid a multitude of lies in every word of our dialogue. How could I tell her my parents were in a frenzy trying to make sense of my actions? I kept the small talk to a minimum and introduced her to my husband. Trip was callous. I excused his disrespect and made light of his curtness.

Why couldn't he just be nice to her? She didn't know what was happening. My brief exchange with her was light. Every encounter in the past week had been heavy, and in this instance, I overlooked the pain that was now my companion.

I waved goodbye and continued down the aisle and she went in the opposite direction. Trip took the empty suit case that he was carrying and hit me in the back of my knees, causing my legs to buckle. I was embarrassed. I was hurt. Did he really think it was my fault?

Trip was in between jobs so it seemed like a good time to relocate. We had just returned from a job hunting Trip visiting many states in the Union looking for a place to settle. One night, I came out of the hotel bathroom in tears.

"Look," I said, fighting to steady my voice and handing him the pregnancy wand. "I'm pregnant."

Trip stood speechless, half smiling. Silence loomed between us. Then his eyes inflated and his half smile turned to a frown as he sat hard into a chair. "I told you I didn't want to have a child," he said.

Having children would draw us into society and away from the religious escape we planned, but I couldn't deny I longed for a son.

"I didn't either," I said, aiming to show him we were on the same page in hopes he wouldn't take his anger out on me. I couldn't tell him what I really felt. I was happy, frightened and angry. Happy because I was going to have his baby, frightened because I knew it was not what he wanted, and angry because I was giving him a gift and he didn't see it that way!

"It takes two to tango, Trip," I retorted. Trip rose from the chair and walked over to me with sullen eyes.

"I thought you wanted a spiritual life, not a worldly one," he said.

I stepped back an arm's distance away from him. "I don't understand why you can't accept that perhaps God wanted us to have a child. We got pregnant using protection."

"You got pregnant, not me," he said.

I reached for the bed to brace myself, my eyes fluttering in disbelief. I couldn't believe he was denying me. I was holding his child! I mustered the strength and reminded him.

"The book of Psalms says, 'Children are a heritage from the Lord, offspring a reward from Him.'" He said nothing.

Things were changing — or were they? Maybe things were already as they were and my eyes were opening. This had happened only a month before we decided to leave our families.

It was noon when Trip pulled the Ryder truck out of the driveway. I followed in our car. We took a circuitous route to make sure no one would follow us. We drove an hour out of our way and stopped in another Gold Rush town before making our way over the Sierra.

We could relax now. No one knew our business here. I took a deep breath, noticing I hadn't done so in days. In some ways I felt a sense of freedom. Whatever I said to anyone from here on would be my reality. I didn't have to explain myself to anyone anymore. Maybe I could move forward and forget my pain and find answers. My family now was Trip and our baby. I found comfort in that.

We picked up some snacks and drinks for the road at a gas station and hit the road. Trip was still in front of me and managed to make the traffic light, but I didn't. I watched him drive down the road. I expected he would notice that I wasn't behind him and he'd pull over. He didn't. *I'll catch up.* I thought.

The light turned green and I headed after him. *Surely he's just ahead on the side of the road waiting for me.* I thought.

I drove five miles and still no Ryder truck anywhere. Finally, in the lane coming toward me, I spotted the crayon yellow of a truck peering over the crowd of automobiles. As the truck got closer, I saw Trip wearing his Vuarnet sunglasses and dark T-shirt in the driver's seat; he was coming back for me. I was ecstatic. As soon as I could, I pulled over, made a U-turn and followed in the direction he supposedly drove. I went back to the gas station because that was where we were last together, but I didn't see him anywhere. I drove around town and then back down the road where I had first spotted him. There was no sign of him. I went up and down that stretch of road for forty-five minutes. Now I was nervous. *What if I don't find him? Where could he have gone? What could have happened to him?*

Nightfall was coming and the baby growing in my belly needed my attention. I went back to the gas station and asked the attendant if he remembered us. He was a young man in his early twenties, with a medium muscular frame and confident demeanor. Dirty blond hair fell to his shoulders, covering his dull blue eyes.

"Yeah, I 'member the Ryder truck, but I haven't seen it since."

I looked around, folded my arms then unfolded them to pat the sides of my thighs. "Well, could you tell me where the nearest hotel is?"

"Sure thing," he said, then proceeded to give me directions.

"Thank you so much," I said. "May I ask another favor?"

"And what's that?" he said with a smile.

"If my husband returns here, would you let him know where I'm staying?"

"You bet," he said with a reassuring nod of his head.

I thanked him again and got something to eat.

I found the hotel the attendant had recommended and with a few belongings and my dinner, I checked in. By now, I felt sick. I wasn't sure if it was from the pregnancy or from the uncertainty of what I was going to do.

Inside my hotel room, I set up a little dining spot and forced myself to eat. A rap at the door startled me and I bounced up to answer it. With an unsteady hand, I opened the door. There stood Trip. He fell through the threshold onto his knees, half grabbing me, half hugging me.

"I thought I lost you! I thought I lost my family!" He said almost in tears. And in the same breath he raised his voice saying, "How can you relax after I have been looking all over for you?"

"I've been looking for you too," I said, not feeling up to a fight. "I needed to rest and get some energy before I could think about my next step." I paused, then changed the subject. "How did you know I was here?"

"The attendant told me. I went back to the gas station and he told me you were waiting for me here."

Trip paced the floor in deep thought. I crawled up onto the bed and curled up. Finally, Trip said, "You know, Cubby, I thought you had been kidnapped and I would have to go back to your Dad on my hands and knees begging forgiveness. In one swipe, I thought I lost my wife, my family."

He really does want a family. Maybe he's just scared and unsure about having a child like me.

"I thought about what it would be like to walk the painful road of posting 'lost' flyers of you all over town," he continued.

A strange look came over his face. *Did he really wish that that had happened?*

The next day we headed east, over the Sierra and into Nevada. There was nothing before us, only open land and new places. Before we knew it, we crossed the border into Idaho. It had only been a few days but leaving California seemed like a lifetime ago. We pulled into a restaurant in Twin Falls. It was a welcome break from driving alone. I stretched my legs and looked north in the direction where Montana lay. I stood erect. The sky hovered with black clouds. And like the sense of an unseen presence in the room, an eerie sensation came over me, urging me not to go there.

"Trip, do you think we could stay in Idaho for a while? I'm not really sure I want to press on to Montana just yet. It has been a difficult couple of weeks and I'm tired."

He seemed to be okay with the idea. I guess Idaho was far enough away for him. At least for now.

Idaho

The Drysdales stood outside their home waiting to meet us. I stood alongside Trip, my hands cupped around his arm which he held bent at his waist as if by condition. We were possible renters. I wore remnants of our life in California, fitted white jeans with a white T-shirt designed by a Bay Area artist with white stilettos; quite the contrast from what people wore in the heart of Idaho potato country. Trip looked more suitable in Wrangler jeans and a T-shirt. He was good at charming people with his appearance, standing at 6 feet 3 inches with a five o'clock shadow and blue eyes.

Trip's mom owned a women's boutique in Rancho Murieta, back in California. Trip kept the books. His mom ran the store and I helped from time to time. We purchased unique lines of clothes that both Trip's mom and I loved even for ourselves. I was the doll Trip loved to dress.

We looked like the perfect couple, a sure bet for any landlord.

"I reckon you can move in when'er yer ready," Mr. Drysdale said.

We settled into our new life and continued trading our possessions for treasures in heaven. We had a house full of nice furniture and boutique clothes with which we needed to part. We briefly talked about selling our things before we left

California, but Trip thought it would be best to go as soon as possible and disperse our goods when we settled. What we didn't sell, we sought out poorer folk to whom we gave our alms. Trip had some money to his name also, all of which he insisted on keeping. That was interesting to me.

"It sounds a little worldly, don't you think? Not spiritual." I said.

"What's worldly?"

"We give things away but not the money."

"We'll invest the money and watch it grow so we can live humbly off it," he explained. "I'll find seasonal or temporary work to avoid establishing roots then use that money to make ends meet."

We met Robert from Edward Jones and decided to invest the money with him. Robert reminded me of Kevin Costner in *Dances with Wolves*; tall, slender, blondish-brown hair with blue eyes. The movie was playing in theaters that winter and we went to see it.

Trip and I did everything together, even though we had problems in our marriage. We were sojourners and I enjoyed our life together. I feared, though, how Trip would treat me after the baby was born. *Would he completely push me away?*

"Damn it, Cubby! How am I going to keep my money from depleting if God doesn't bless my investments?"

"Why do you think God should bless your investments?

"Because we're giving up everything to find Him and He should bless us."

I could see why he might think that, but I didn't see how that necessarily made the issues congruent.

"Maybe you're looking at it wrong."

"What?"

"Just because your investments are not making money, doesn't mean that God is not with us."

He shrugged.

I put my arms around my beautiful husband, believing he could do anything. He had so many innate gifts. I wondered why he couldn't see what I saw. With my arms around him I gently said, "Don't lose heart."

Trip went to work for The Dellsworth Potato Company. Old man Dellsworth was a jovial man with a rotund belly. He was happy to have a businessman from California join his team, but it perplexed him when Trip turned down the desk job to work as a laborer. "There's less entanglement with a simple job," Trip said, dressed in his Wranglers and open flannel that covered a T-shirt. It was fall. We continued to give away almost everything we had. Winter was hinting that it was on its way.

When Christmas came, I was six months pregnant. It was my first Christmas without a tree, presents, and a big holiday feast, and the first holiday without my family. I felt a familiar pain place its weight on my shoulders—the same emotion I had felt when I said goodbye to my family. It remained my companion.

We went for a walk on Christmas Eve. Trip and I walked the frozen streets of the neighborhood alone, watching the crystal ice droplets fall. I contemplated the holiday lights shining within nearby homes. How I missed my family. Everyone in the neighborhood joyfully celebrated the season. People were having parties, gatherings, and exchanging baked goods and gifts. I could hear laughter and singing.

Trip had researched Christmas before we met and discovered that in fact, Christmas was a pagan holiday, from the time of year, to the tree adorned with idols, to the virgin birth. When Christianity grew in numbers and power, its leaders superimposed their traditions on the already existing holy days in order to attract converts. He concluded that Christianity couldn't be a true religion if it took what already existed and peddled it for its own profits.

Just after Christmas, my little brother came to stay with us. He was the only family member that we didn't say goodbye to. Trip admired my little brother's courage to drop out of college to become a sojourner and attributed our grand decision to leave family to him. So Trip decreed that he was okay to be a part of our lives.

"Hey, how's my sis?" he asked as he grabbed me and gave me a big squeeze. "I've been roaming the Earth a while and felt it was a good time to come visit"

"Please stay with us," I asked. "It's so good to have family around."

"I have nowhere that's calling me at the moment. Why not," He said with a warm smile.

I felt safe having my brother around. When we were little, my brother and I played together a lot. It always seemed to be us two, mostly; maybe because we were the youngest of the family. Now in the middle of January in Western Idaho, the winter season didn't feel so cold. We spent a lot of time going for walks when Trip was at work.

"So how's it going sis?"

"Things are going. I feel so happy to be pregnant."

"How are things with Trip?"

"Good."

"Honestly now. How are you?"

"Honestly, things are a little rough sometimes. Trip doesn't seem to have much compassion for me now that I'm pregnant. I don't know. Maybe not even before I was pregnant. It's hard to tell."

"Maybe he's just nervous about becoming a father," he paused. "Either way, don't forget about you, Sis. You're pretty special," he added as he side-hugged me and we kept walking.

My little brother stayed with us for a couple of weeks. Although Trip had welcomed him into our home, I could sense that he wished he hadn't.

"Well, I think we did the right thing, leaving our families and giving away our things," Trip said with self-satisfaction.

"I don't know if leaving the family is really the issue," my brother replied. "I think the issue might be more to do with searching your heart and following it. It's more standing up for yourself despite what others say."

Tension began to mount between my brother and Trip. Trip didn't like people disagreeing with him. He had difficulty hearing another view.

My brother left and said he'd return after the baby was born.

Spring came with the intermittent dusting of snow flurries. It was March, and with the birth of nature's new life came the birth of my son. It was one of the most vivid days of my life. I didn't feel so without family anymore; I was beginning my own. The awesome responsibility of presenting to the world a commendable man who would contribute to society fell heavy on my heart. Still, it was a precious burden I eagerly accepted. I had a son to love from the man I adored.

Two days later we brought him home from the hospital. Trip was happy that I was now back to take care of his needs.

"Why don't you make us some dinner?" he said not five minutes after our arrival.

I reluctantly began to make dinner and all at once began to shake uncontrollably. Tears streamed down my face as my muscles turned to noodles. Trip caught me before I hit the floor.

"I told you having a baby would only take us away from a spiritual life," he said, placing me in a chair. "Instead of focusing on each other and finding truth, we have to take care of the baby."

"Why do you blame me? Can't you see that our son is a gift?

"Because I chose you."

My heart leaped.

"I didn't choose to have a baby."

My heart sank. "Then why didn't you have the balls to get a vasectomy if you didn't want children?"

I saw his hand fly toward my face then fall to the back of his neck.

The air in the kitchen became heavy and then he spoke. "Well, maybe that's what I need to do. Maybe we can still make this journey with only one child. We can control one little life," he mused.

I was relieved to know he could give things rational thought. No one spoke for a while then I sheepishly asked.

"Trip," I said without lifting my eyes. "I'm thrashed from giving birth. Do you think you could find it in your heart to help me recover?" Before he could answer, someone knocked at the door. He went to answer it. It was the Drysdales and other neighbors offering help.

I overheard the conversation from the kitchen. Trip was telling them we didn't need anything, but before he could shut the door, I yelled from inside saying,

"Thank you. Yes, we would greatly appreciate anything."

The following week we were showered with meals and helping hands. Mrs. Drysdale even gave me a hand-made blanket for Kuder which I still keep safe to this day. I don't know if they ever realized how great a deed they did for me. Trip showed me no compassion. I endured postpartum alone, except for the kindness of my neighbors.

My little brother did return just after Kuder was born.

"Hey, Sis! I'm back!" He said as I opened the door. I jumped into his arms and squeezed him tight.

"You're here! I'm so happy to see you! Come!" I said taking his hand and pulling him into the bedroom. "I want you to meet your nephew, Kuder."

"Wow . . . Kuder . . . Hi little one." He said as he approached him lying on the bed. "Can I pick him up?"

"Of course! Here, let me hand him to you." I gently scooped up Kuder and placed him in his arms.

"He sure is cute. How did you come up with that name? It's kinda weird, not gonna lie."

"Well, he's actually named after Trip. So Kuder is now the fourth in the long line of Thaddeuses. But honestly, the name doesn't fit him. I can't see him taking after that lineage. Don't tell Trip I said that."

"You know I won't," he said, looking up at me as he gently rocked Kuder.

I continued my animated explanation, acting it out. "Anyway, so I would go around the house saying he was the cutest baby! I'd say 'cutest baby, cutest baby!' Cutest baby turned into Cuder baby which then turned into simply Kuder. So, I started calling him Kuder, and Trip did, too."

"Yeah, sounds like you," he said with a smile as he looked at Kuder.

It was lovely to share my son with my little brother. But he only stayed a few days. One day, while my brother was out buying some supplies, Trip shared some concerns with me.

"Kuder doesn't look like me."

"What do you mean? He has your nose, your mouth, and your eyes," I rebutted.

"No matter what, I'll raise the child as if he was mine, but I think we should have a paternity test done."

"What?!" He might as well have punched me in the gut. "You, you think I've been unfaithful?"

"No, but your little brother has been staying with us. He's not married, doesn't have a girlfriend. You know he has to jack off in the bathroom. He spends a lot of time in there. Maybe while you took a bath and his sperm got into you? Sperm can live outside the body, ya know."

"You're disgusting!" I felt violated. "How can you say such a thing? I was pregnant before my brother came to stay with us!"

"Yeah, but my sperm could've died out and been replaced with his."

"Do you know how ridiculous you sound?"

We went to see my obstetrician and Trip confessed his paternity doubts to him.

"You know Doc, the baby doesn't really look like me."

"Really? I see a lot of you in him. He's adorable."

"He looks more like her. What if I'm not the father? Her brother was staying with us for a while. Maybe his sperm lived in the bathroom and got into her."

The doctor's face was incredulous and he said without emotion. "You know sperm can't live outside the body for more than fifteen to thirty minutes with the best of conditions. In water, significantly less, if at all."

As he spoke, the absurdity of Trip's concern resonated off the walls in the doctor's office, and it was obvious to all of us that paternity was not the issue but the realization of fatherhood falling heavily on his shoulders.

I never told my brother about Trip's ridiculous accusation.

"Sis, I'm leaving. I don't belong with you guys and I don't really trust Trip. He always has to be right," he hugged me. "Be careful."

"I'll be okay." I smiled gently. "Thank you for everything," I said as I hugged him hard. "Where will you go?"

"I'll find my way. You take care of yourself and the baby." He looked down at Kuder and caressed his face. "He sure is cute."

Sorrow filled my heart. I had hoped my little brother would stay with us so I could hold onto one family member.

"Don't look so sad. We'll see each other soon."

He kissed my cheek and hugged me tight. "Tell Trip 'bye for me."

I nodded. He picked up his bag and walked out the door, down the street.

He went his way, back and forth to my family back home while Trip and I pushed further away into darkness.

∽

April came with the spring thaw. It was time to head toward Montana. We had begun to feel too comfortable, too attached to Idaho, to the Drysdales, to a life so easily made for us.

"We can't stay here any longer," Trip told the Drysdales.

"Why? Everythin's been goin' so well for ya'll here," Mrs. Drysdale said.

"Old man Dellsworth ain't given ya a hard time, is he?" Mr. Drysdale teased.

"Well, with all due respect, we are on a quest to find truth and need to find a place conducive to that," Trip said.

"Why, the Mormon Church has the truth. Ya came to the right place." Mr. Drysdale said with a grand smile.

'That's just it. You don't have it. No one does. Every religion says they do and all practice the same things just called by different names. We don't want to be trapped in your ignorance," Trip explained.

The conversation that followed turned into a heated argument as religious conversations tend to do. And as all religious people can't do—hear another's side—Trip dusted his hands from the place that did not receive his words.

"You're a fool," Mr. Drysdale said as he turned away shaking his head.

Why he didn't tell the Dellsworth's to go to hell as well, I'll never know. Instead we collected Trip's last paycheck.

I pressed my face against the passenger window, straining to see Mr. Dellsworth. He looked bewildered. We used to drive a sedan, now we drove a half-ton pickup truck.

Trip bought a red Chevy truck thinking we would eventually live out of the back. "It's perfect!" he said. "Soon we'll get a camper with all our worldly possessions inside and live off the land!"

The idea scared me, but I was willing to try. My family never camped. One of my brothers put it this way, "We already grew up poor. Why would I want to pretend I don't have anything? Sleep on the ground, no shelter, dirt in my food. No thanks!"

We got out of the truck to say goodbye. Mr. Dellsworth stared at us as though we were strangers. He looked at Trip, who now wore a full beard. Trip said men were supposed to have facial hair and not shave so not to be like women.

Mr. Dellsworth cast his eyes to me. He stared at my shoes, followed up my legs, onto my chest to rest his gaze on my eyes. He looked into me expressing sorrow and regret. "What happened to those stilettos and California outfits?" I read in his eyes.

Townsend

The sun shone bright the day we left Idaho; the air still hinted of winter not far behind. Thousands of multi-colored butterflies filled the spring sky tenderly assaulting us as we loaded into the cars. We drove out of the driveway as if we were going to the grocery store. No one waved goodbye or said good luck. Only butterflies came to bid us farewell. Trip drove the half-ton truck filled with our remaining belongings: a queen bed, Kuder's crib, a futon, pots and pans, a desk, a bookcase for his books, and the oversized computer chair. I drove the sedan with our clothes. This time, Kuder was with me.

We drove long stretches of road through nature for miles on end. Guided by rivers through vast plains, we found ourselves cradled by the majestic Montana mountains, thunderous white peaks sprawling snow onto the plains like a bride who spreads her wedding dress before she walks down the aisle. Montana was frighteningly unfamiliar, yet her grandeur captivated me. Townsend sat amid this expanse, a small town of about 2,000 people.

We had no plans for a final destination so we decided to look here. We hoped to rent something, but a small house on a cul-de-sac caught our eye. We stepped into a realtor's office and learned the price was $9,000! Trip cut a check and the little two-bedroom home on a quarter-acre was ours.

"Wow! We could never find a deal like this in California," Trip said. "Now I know we are being blessed."

"Blessed?" I questioned.

"Yeah, we did the right thing by leaving our families."

"How can you assume that? Good fortune doesn't necessarily equate to God being with us. What if something doesn't go our way? Does that mean God is against us?"

"No. Anyway, that can't happen. We've sold almost everything or given it away and left our families. God has to be on our side."

"Maybe it's what we make of our situations, not that blessing equals God's approval and no blessing His disapproval?"

"What? That doesn't make sense," he said, waving me off as if I were an annoying fly. Deep down I knew I was right. I didn't press, though.

We had our own little piece of the world now. We made the house ours by removing carpets and anything else that wasn't nailed down. We spent weeks ridding the property of cigarette butts, broken beer bottles, and caked in trash. Although the home was virtually empty, the garage was stuffed with debris. We managed to salvage an antique baseball mitt and an old plastic tootsie roll cylinder filled with glass marbles. We had the land, a small house, and privacy, no mortgage, no landlord, and no entanglement with the 'world'. Our plan to live off a garden and fruit trees while Trip fished could begin.

Catch and release was Trip's first love. As a small boy, he spent many vacations in Montana with his grandfather, who taught him how to fly fish. His grandfather's family immigrated to Butte, Montana, from Serbia generations before. Now Trip fished in the playground of his youth.

We met our next door neighbors soon after we moved in. The Cumminghams were an elderly couple whose children and grandchildren didn't live nearby. He was a World War II veteran. Mr. Cunningham was well over six feet tall with broad shoulders. He walked with a muscular gait resembling a strong young man. His hair had gone silver and his eyelids folded over his brown eyes to reveal a twinkle. He told stories that saluted an era of honor.

"It was midnight," Mr. Cunningham recalled, "pourin' rain, no one was at the train station to meet me, no one knew I was comin' home. The malaria I contracted in Africa came back. I was shiverin' with fever and drenched to the bone, but God I didn't care! I was home again on American soil. So happy I was I kissed the ground beneath ma' feet. So many ma' friends didn't make it back," he said sadly then continued.

"It's so differ'nt now with the vets from Desert Storm. The entire town knows they're comin' home; a whole mess of people wait at the train and a parade downtown, not for the group of soldiers, but for each one that returns. Most of these boys were only gone a few months and never saw a battle."

For four long years, Mr. Cunningham saw nothing but battle.

"A lot of vets of Desert Storm complained of post-traumatic stress and they receive assistance for this condition. Forty-five years ago, no one complained of post-traumatic nothin', we just dealt with whatev'r," Mr. Cunningham continued, not understanding the present state of the Union.

Mrs. Cunningham wore her chestnut-dyed hair short, tightly

curled to her head. She, too, had big brown eyes, her eyelids only hinting at her age. She was a happy woman, always smiling. She had a petite frame but was not delicate. She had a gruff way about her, but she was never offensive. She had stories of her own.

"I was married and pregnant when the war started. He went off to war too, but came home in a box."

"Oh, I'm sorry," I whispered.

"You heard of the Battle of the Bulge?"

We nodded.

"That's where he was killed"

Trip and I didn't know how to respond.

"Well, anyway, I had Curtis and raised him on my own until I met up with Dick."

"How did you meet?" I asked, sensing that changing the subject would be welcomed.

"We all knew each other, growing up in the same town and all," Mr. Cunningham said.

"Yeah, after the war, we met up at a town dance. Things went well and we got married." Mrs. Cunningham added.

Her son kept his father's name, the flag that draped over his coffin and his medals in honor of his memory. "It's the least I could do for ma fallen comrade," Mr. Cunningham confessed with sorrow yet pride.

The Cunningham's were the closest semblance of socializing I enjoyed in all my years with Trip. Their stories of days gone by were captivating. They were the stories of two souls who had lived through great tragedy and triumph; rough around the edges, but refined at heart. The Cunningham's weren't religious nor did we ever speak of religion with them.

Trip never found work in Townsend, although Mr. Cunningham offered to help him find a job. "Thanks, but that's okay," Trip replied.

When the numbers in the bank account began to dwindle, he had to think about a job. The idea of being self-sufficient sounded good, but reality proved to have other bills for which living off the land could not pay. The possibility of me working outside the home was not an option. My place was "with the boy" and I was honored to have that job. Kuder was a gift. That's how we happened upon the Cook Mansion. Real estate seemed lucrative.

There it sat just outside Townsend on Hwy 287, 8,000 square feet, stately in its 1914 grandeur. We tossed around the idea of opening a bed and breakfast to make ends meet.

"I've never seen you want something so much as this house," Trip said surprised.

"Please Trip, let's do this. We could be self-employed, self-sufficient without depleting the money."

"I don't know," he thought for a moment then continued. "My heart would be consumed with running a business and I won't have time to study scripture or fish. It will draw us away from God."

My conscience stung, but I said what I was thinking anyway. "We need to do something to make money. I would love to serve people in our home. You get to fish. Can't I do something I like, too?"

"I thought you were a spiritual woman," he said, disgusted. "Fly fishing brings us food and being out in nature brings me closer to God. We have to focus on the next life if we're going to find truth, not fancy homes and house guests."

"But Trip, wait, we-" Trip got in my face and finished my sentence.

"—We need to be sojourners, without a country, without a home."

Oh no! My thoughts raced. *Trip is using God for his own convenience. This isn't the way of truth! But I love him.* And the revelation disappeared as quickly as it came.

We spent afternoons walking in circles around our one-car garage, trying to decide what to do next. I remember seeing the Cunninghams looking out their window with puzzled looks on their faces.

"Hey, I just made some cookies. Would you like to come over later?" Mrs. Cunningham asked, poking her head out the back door.

"Maybe," Trip replied, not breaking stride around the garage.

The bed and breakfast was no longer an option, and the path of our spiritual destination came into question. Should we continue making the house our own? Could we make a life here? What about living in the truck? What would be the next step to bring us closer to truth? Out of our walks encircling the garage came our next step; it was the day when we threw away our family pictures.

"We need to show we've left our past for a new future," Trip said.

First to hit the trash can were pictures of our wedding. The day he promised to love me as Christ loved the church giving his life in exchange for mine. With one heave the evidence of our wedding was gone. He seemed relieved.

Next on the chopping block was me. He stood over the trash taking my wedding picture out of its frame. Without a second look or a thought of hesitation he tore me into pieces and shattered the frame. I turned away and looked at the ground.

I thought of the attachment he had to the pictures of Donna. I found them in his Stanford yearbook during our first year of marriage. She had long blond hair with a pretty smile. He kept her pictures safely on its page, something he dismissed as just an old girlfriend who no longer meant anything. In the same breath he confessed he had three shoe boxes of her correspondence. When I suggested letting those things go, he kicked the door and put the pictures and letters away.

"Hey Cubby, did you hear me?" Trip said. "We'll only keep pictures of you and me that fit into our new family album." I composed myself, looked back at him and nodded.

"Okay, what's next?" he asked, not expecting an answer. He gathered the pictures of his brothers, mom and dad, took one look, tore them and threw them in the trash. He flipped through his soccer pictures, glanced at a few and sighed. Slowly, he let them fall. He looked at me. It was my turn.

I gave him pictures of my childhood, my photo album of Spain and my dance videos.

The Christian church I attended before I met Trip advised me against dance. Church leaders said dancing, although done in the Old Testament by King David to express joy, is different from contemporary dance done for evil and sexual motives. This was a great internal contention with me. Why if I was created in God's image to love dance, would it be wrong? I danced on the USC dance team for three years before I gave it up for the sake of spiritual insight.

Next was my family. I hesitated, and with a heavy heart, I handed him the pictures, withholding one. He tore them with purpose.

"Can't I keep these?" I asked. "I was only five."

I had a series of pictures of me with my Dad. We were in a photo booth found at malls and fun parks, where you draw the curtain and the camera takes rapid fire photos. My Dad and I were making faces and snuggling.

"You were your Daddy's little girl and you need to let that go. Just cut your Dad out of the pictures. Besides, it's you and me now, Cubby," he said.

I went through all four of the pictures carefully cutting my Dad from those photos. I stared at the severed pieces of his face that fell onto my lap. I held back my tears not wanting to elicit Trip's anger. He took the pieces and added them to the contents of the trash. With one swipe of his hands as if brushing off dirt, he was satisfied with the day's accomplishments.

The white thunderous peaks had receded now to reveal green plains bustling with new life. From horizon to horizon, white clouds dotted the pristine blue sky and every third or fourth day the clouds would accumulate to cool the expanse with commanding thundershowers. And as the sky would clear, every star that had ever been created seemed to appear in the ebony dome of the night sky. It was July in Montana and we were still debating what to do with our house while making plans for Kuder's four-month check-up.

We took him for his second set of shots, but something went wrong. Before we went, he was laughing, babbling, smiling and almost crawling. When we got home, he was a lump. We called the doctor and he said it was normal after shots to experience some side effects, but "not to worry"; he would recover with time. He did recover, but for months he wouldn't smile. It took a lot of coaxing to get him to laugh again. His first shots he only reacted with a fever. We wondered if the vaccinations might have caused this lapse in Kuder.

"Cubby," Trip began as if lecturing to a large crowd, attention he always longed for. "You know the world wants to lull us to sleep, to believe there is no heaven or hell, and to get us to think we are in control when in fact we aren't. According to my studies in the book of Revelation, the devil is supposed to be released in the last days, at which time he will be allowed to have total control of the world before the second coming. I think that time is now. What if the government uses vaccinations to dumb us down?"

"Are you suggesting the government did this?" I asked.

"What if the government wanted to control its people without them knowing? What if they laced the vaccinations with drugs to make us dull, too apathetic to think, or to question our leaders? What better way to do it than under the cover of national health? Parents would never question getting their children vaccinated."

"So you think Satan is in control of the government?"

"We know from the Old Testament that Satan has been bound since he was banished for wanting to be God, then promised complete reign during the end of days. I think he was released in the mid-1800s, when man began industrialization. When men tend the earth, leading simple lives, their faith is that of a child, as Jesus said we must have. The more man creates, the more he draws away from God. Women, too, question the divine order of being under men. Think about it. There was a time when we were not taxed for property and then came income tax, which people swore would never happen. Then the crash of '29 followed by the Depression and President Roosevelt who shoved government deeper into our lives creating what is now known as welfare. And our social security number, the mark of the beast. We're now being monitored with nine digits. Under the pretext of the government, Satan is gaining control. So it isn't so difficult to think that the government would take the next step."

"Come on!! What you're saying is pretty serious."

"We know that Satan has penetrated the church. No one's really different. No one has power. No one really loves his neighbor as himself, like Jesus commands if we are saved. It only makes sense that Satan would spread his domain. That's why we chose this path. We have been given eyes to see that something is not right and we hope that God will honor his promise that those who seek will find and He will give to those who ask and that finally the door of heaven will be opened to us."

October came, hinting that the harsh Montana winter would not be far behind. Our little house on the cul-de-sac was now completely gutted, a shell, not enough to protect us through the long months. Up until this point, we vacillated. Some days we'd decide to make the house ours and other days, Trip questioned whether it was the right thing to do. I just wanted some stability, a place to start over, but we had to keep otherworldly to follow that which we pursued. The only question that remained now that winter was coming, was if we would find a place to live during the cold of winter and continue working on the house in the spring or was it time to sell and start again?

It was time to go, again. I wasn't that surprised, but I really wanted to stay in Townsend and make a life there.

The moving sale rid us of the few belongings we still had. Trip even managed to part with the bookcase and desk and I ceded Kuder's crib and the blankets I had made for him. We left the cul-de-sac with a futon, pots and pans, and the oversized computer chair. The serenity of Townsend, Montana and the generosity it had shown could not convince us to stay. The hope that God was on our side by giving us a $9,000 house changed into the idea that it was Satan posing to be gracious only to captivate us in the 'world' by keeping us from our pursuit.

We said goodbye to the Cunninghams. Mr. Cunningham did not understand why we would abandon what we started and not make a life next door. Mrs. Cunningham grew attached to Kuder, but never said a word with respect to our leaving. She only had regret in her eyes. This was the only time I saw Trip sad to leave someone. And with our departure went the hope of a simple life, a place of our own, and it was confirmation that Trip and God were at odds.

West Yellowstone

A middle-aged woman with frayed, salt-and-peppered hair sat knitting behind the hotel's front desk. She looked up from her work to feast her eyes on the hunk of a man standing before her: 220 pounds of manliness; tall, like the lodgepole pines that landscaped the town, he stood booted in black Sorels. A smirk drew across her cheeks as her dim eyes devoured the handsome stranger. Aware of his charm, Trip rested a bent elbow on the counter.

"How much are your rooms for two and a baby?"

"Vacationing?" she asked, following her forefinger with her eyes across the counter to find the price. "$39 a night."

"Actually, we just got into town and are looking for a place to stay."

Her eyes fluttered and the smirk grew to a smile as color returned to her pale cheeks. "Really, this must be your lucky day. Hi! I'm Mrs. Morgan!" she said as she reached out her hand to shake Trip's. She didn't even acknowledge me.

"We have a little house for rent just outside of town. I'll take you there," she continued.

A subdivision of vacation homes sat eight miles out of West Yellowstone on Highway 20. Nestled in the shadow of the large log house of Mrs. Morgan, her five children and her husband, sat a cozy one-room suite completely furnished with antiques left by the previous owners. I fell in love with the place and it became our new home.

Mr. Morgan stood a third of Trip's size, smaller even than Mrs. Morgan. Meek. It made sense why Mrs. Morgan drooled over Trip whenever she was in his presence. The Morgan's and a bed and breakfast were the only year round residents in the subdivision, and with the addition of us, made three inhabited buildings.

Trip found employment doing odd jobs for the bed and breakfast. The business had a small clientele, which the owners could manage, and eventually the work ended, but not before we met Bell.

Bell was an eighty-year-old woman who needed help removing the snow drift that threatened her roof. The owner of the bed and breakfast asked Trip if he wanted to help her.

"Hey Cubby, here's a chance to help a person in need. God should notice, don't you think?" Trip asked, hoping to get on God's good side.

I liked the idea. It was a chance to meet someone, anyone, as socializing happened less and less.

Bell lived alone and never left her home all winter long, and rarely did she venture off her property, even in the spring when she wasn't landlocked from the snow. A local woman delivered supplies to her, and as I got to know her, I brought her goodies she craved for which she wouldn't have asked.

Bell sat on a small fortune of one hundred acres that stretched up the mountainside. She inherited the homestead from her aunt and uncle. She and her sister came to live with them when their parents died from the influenza epidemic in the early 1900s. Bell's sister married, as did she, but Bell's husband died of a heart attack when she was a young bride, bringing her back to live with her aunt and uncle. At twenty-nine, she was diagnosed with kidney disease and given a grim prognosis. Fifty-one years later when I came to know her, hints of a brunette with fiery blue eyes greeted me. And although her small stature was frail, she was as feisty as a school-girl.

Mother Nature never ceased to show her beauty in the northern country. Sometimes before the full breadth of a storm, the snow floated down onto a still landscape, as long as no snowmobilers were vacationing. Kuder and I went for walks on those unique days, listening to the sound of silence and marveling at the intimidating grandeur of the Rockies buffeted by angelic snow. Most days, though, the storms blew horizontal winds, burying homes in twenty-foot snow drifts while forty below could be expected this time of year. Twilight began at 3:00 p.m., giving daylight little chance to comfort. During the long season of short days, Trip introduced another revelation.

"We're going to change the Sabbath to Saturdays," Trip said.

"Why?"

"Maybe the house in Townsend was a clue letting us know we're not on the right track. What was I thinking? We can't own a house and be otherworldly."

"It seems to me the house in Townsend was a lack of follow through on our part, having nothing to do with being on the right track."

"What do you know?"

I didn't understand how he always equated good fortune to God being with us. Life was life to me, and one's fortune or misfortune came from the good or bad view one chose to take. I could see his side, but saw that if a person continued to believe like that, it would only spiral into a pit of constant second guessing oneself while life slipped away. But I chose not to say anymore. I knew it would fall on deaf ears.

He walked to the window, looking out onto the blanket of snow overshadowed by blistering winds, and began to speak again.

"If Christianity doesn't have the truth then we should go back to its roots in Judaism. Our religious forefathers could have lost the path a long time ago. It's possible we could pick it up where they went astray."

From Friday sundown to Saturday evening we did nothing. All Kuder and I could do was hear Trip lecture and break for meals; no playing with Kuder, no making the beds, not even replacing a fallen pillow. I couldn't even use the excuse to make dinner when I could no longer listen. I had prepared all of the meals and beverages we would consume, I prepared on Friday before dusk. Saturday nights came as a blessing just to do the dishes. Pots and pans clamoring in the sink amidst the running water was a welcome reprieve from Trip's voice.

"Why don't we attend a Jewish Sabbath if we are following Judaism? Food shared is twice blessed," I offered.

"That's a bad idea. They'll just drag us off our journey."

"What? So we can follow their traditions yet assume they are wrong? That doesn't make sense."

"Yeah, we are sojourners. They aren't."

A large hotel, restaurant, and KOA shared space in the compound that sat across from the subdivision. Mr. Morgan managed the hotel and was kind enough to help Trip get a job as a dishwasher at the adjacent restaurant. Among Trip's coworkers was a young blond waitress with whom Trip formed an affinity. I thought of the picture I found of Donna, how he carefully stored her portrait safely among his things. Like Donna, this waitress had long blond hair and a beautiful smile.

"Do you wish I was blond?"

"You're pretty, for a Mexican."

My heart fell to my stomach, crushed that the man I adored thought so little of me. To him, I would never be more than a laborer's daughter.

My father had worked in the orchards of California and allowed us to experience the hardship of manual labor to recognize the value of an education. All seven of us went to college, and most of us graduated with prestigious degrees. Why couldn't Trip appreciate that? I tried to conceal my disappointment, but my face betrayed me.

"What's the matter?"

I barely heard his question. My thoughts raced. Why should I be shocked? I sensed his contempt, but couldn't bring myself to admit it. Feeling a spark of self-respect, I reminded myself that I was elected homecoming queen, I attended USC and studied abroad, and had competed on the dance team and Trip hadn't been my only serious boyfriend. I spoke. "I wouldn't mind so much that you're sweet on the girl, if you'd allow me the same freedoms."

"You're a woman and you're supposed to submit to however I lead."

Emotion rushed from my heart to my mouth like the wakes of a passing speedboat. "Yeah, but you're *first* supposed to love your wife as Christ loved the Church and gave Himself up for her! It's the man's responsibility to treat a woman right then the wife would surely follow! If she doesn't, you have every right to complain, but I have been more than kind and submitted to your leadership despite the fact that you treat me like trash! And I have done this because I love you!"

Tears streamed down my face. I was unable to keep up with the flow of emotion. "All my life I have served my brothers and Dad and I know what it's like to be properly treated in return, but you are not fair! My brothers don't even claim to be religious like you!"

"Hold your tongue woman or I'll hold it for you."

Yeah, whatever, I thought. At this point I didn't care what he said. I thought I couldn't remarry. And Trip reminded me that going back to my family would surely land me in hell. But fire and brimstone was not the outcome for leaving him, so I devised a plan to rid myself of him. I would take Kuder with me and together we'd go to the Dakotas. The plains seemed like a good place to start over. I could see myself single and I could see myself raising Kuder on my own.

Trip mostly worked night shifts when the tips were better, but sometimes he also took some day shifts. I would wait for the day he worked a long shift during business hours to take Kuder with me to the bus station in West Yellowstone. There I would take money out of the bank, leave the truck, and we would be on our way. All I would take would be our clothes, and those would be easy to pack the morning of our escape.

In the faint distance of time, my heart tugged at me quietly reminding me that, although I momentarily hated him, I loved him.

Days passed; still no option for a good getaway.

Trip came to me, as he often did, bidding me to perform my marital duties. We rarely made love. Even before we left our families, intimacy lacked in our many sexual encounters, as if his body was present, but never his heart. In his arms, I didn't feel beautiful. He didn't notice my silly quirks; he didn't know what made me smile or care what aroused me. Taking time to discover the intimate woman in me was not his job. The only one who had a responsibility was me. I was his "hose bag," as he let slip; a spouse to deposit guilt-free sperm.

Days continued to pass, and with the passing days my period delayed. I thought for sure I was pregnant. I could hear Trip's voice thunder throughout the subdivision. "Woman, you're dragging me more and more into the world with children. How am I going to make it to heaven?"

But I told him of my suspicions anyway. I wanted a second son; but another more fearful part of me didn't want to endure any more rejection.

When the eighteenth day finally brought my cycle, Trip realized he got lucky. He couldn't come that close again, and planned for a vasectomy to end any possibility of more children.

The road to the urologist in Idaho Falls was long and not well traveled. I looked out from the passenger's seat onto the lonely landscape. I turned my eyes to the constant gray sky and remembered the scene in Twin Falls, in the restaurant parking lot. The sky over Montana warned that darkness loomed north. Was it a coincidence?

Trip met with the urologist and set the date. The morning of his procedure, just before taking the Valium he said, "Are you sure you can drive? It's over a two-hour Trip, maybe three. Each way."

"I think I can handle it." I said with confidence.

"Well, what about the baby? Who will tend to his needs on the long trip if you're driving and I'm drugged up?"

I kept getting ready for our trip to the doctor. I looked forward to the outing.

"Well, I don't know. Maybe we shouldn't go." He was slightly pacing now. "It might be too much for you."

"I'll be fine," I assured him.

I stopped what I was doing and waited for him to look at me. I held his eyes in my gaze. I could see the fear in his eyes about what he was about to do with his body. Without a word, only the look between us, he knew I saw him. I felt a certain triumph in that moment. I knew I was strong. He knew I was strong and he knew it was him who was weak.

He never got the vasectomy. The realization that he didn't have the guts to mess with his manhood humbled him and there was no way of hiding it, although he tried. He could no longer use children or pregnancy to push me away.

A glimmer of hope flickered for our relationship. Maybe he could begin to accept our family and the possibility of a life together still existed for us. I believed any relationship could be sweetened if it survived difficult times. I wanted to believe this and I wanted to believe we could be a family. I wanted to be his confidant, to be his solace, his love. I had to try and put away my thoughts of leaving him.

In the early days of June, spring awakens in the Rockies. Wild huckleberries and strawberries rest in the cool underbrush of lodgepole pines. Kuder and I always stopped to pick nature's treats on our many walks. Bell enjoyed these tasty morsels herself so we often saved some for her. Many of our hikes ended at her house.

"Come. Let's go visit Bubbles," Bell suggested. We trekked about fifty yards west from her house to a large rock formation.

"There's Bubbles," she said, pointing to gurgling water coming up from the ground. I looked down to see a small collection of water no bigger than a kiddy pool. I almost didn't notice it. The water was so clear, it was nearly invisible. The rocks, pebbles and even the dirt had no trace of debris, algae or slime often left by water.

"Go ahead, take a drink and give some to Kuder," she said, handing me a plastic avocado colored cup. "My water is so good for you. Surveyors have come to test my Bubbles and say they have never tested a spring so pure. I have the paper to prove it," she boasted.

She stared at the water and I could see I lost her in deep

thought. After a peaceful moment she said, "We used to share Bubbles with the Native Americans who once roamed these mountains. I was little then. They stopped coming through, so many years ago." She paused again, and then added, "If I had to choose a religion, I'd choose their ways. They are so close to nature. You remember all those arrowheads you've seen around my house, don't you?"

I nodded.

"We found lots of them right here near Bubbles." She walked away from the spring back toward the house.

"Come, child. I have something to show you."

Kuder and I caught up to her and walked back to her house in silence. She waved us inside and we followed her to the sill of a large picture window facing the southern sun; the spot where we always sat when we visited her during the non-winter months. "My mountain was under water some time ago," she said as she handed me two brownish gray stones with the imprints of seashells.

"Wow, Bell! Have you ever had these tested?"

"No. I have many artifacts on my land that I don't wish the authorities to know about. Agencies come, take and destroy. These relics are mine to enjoy for now. Soon I will be gone. Let someone else destroy this land when I am no longer here to shed a lone tear." She reached for another rock and said, "Look at this one." giving me a somewhat flat rock the size of a salad plate. "We don't have this kind of foliage at these elevations." My mouth dropped in disbelief. It was a delicate spray of a fern.

"I'm tired now, child. Come see me again soon."

Bell was the only friend I made during my life with Trip.

He allowed Kuder and me to spend uncensored time with her because she was an orphan and a widow, a perfect candidate from whom to score points for heaven.

Autumn in the Rockies is a symphony of sights, sounds and smells. Kuder and I attended the brief event while sitting in silence on boulders within aspen groves. The leaves changed from a spring green to a clear yellow, announcing the vivid glory of fall. The sound of water could be heard, but no stream ran nearby. It was the fall breeze rustling through the aspens, fragrant like the wilderness it cradles, tasting of the Rockies and the sun's warmth that massaged our skin beckoning us to stay just a little longer.

It was on our frequent walks and moments in nature that I found prayer to be easiest. I thanked God for my son, my husband, my life and asked for truth and the humility to recognize it.

Nature's concerto slowed again to its finale leaving no color on the trees and the sun not warm enough to entice us outside. Winter came again to West Yellowstone. It was during the season of blistering winds and short days that Trip tended to hail new ideas.

"Women use their beauty to manipulate men, but the Bible speaks against holding stock in outward appearance. Take the story of the Garden of Eden. Satan tempts Eve first. Why?" Trip asked.

"Adam wasn't there to protect her?" I offered.

Pretending not to hear, he continued. "We'd have to conclude that she is the weaker of the sexes. When she realizes she did the wrong thing, she gets Adam to join her, making him a sinner too. She most likely used her beauty and feminine charms to manipulate him. It seems like throughout the Old Testament women are always trying to get the power men innately have using the one attribute they have: beauty."

"Like?" I asked skeptically.

"Like Samson and Delilah, Jezebel, Bathsheba. Even if you look around today, women are always trying to be men. Women used to wear dresses, now they wear pants. Women can't grow beards, so advertising companies tell men that women find a clean-shaven man more attractive. Scripture advises women against adorning themselves with pearls. She should adorn herself with righteousness."

He stood now looking up to heaven as if receiving a revelation and said. "A good woman is hard to find. Her worth is far above jewels."

I began to wish that I was a man, almost convinced that my gender was inherently wicked. Like a thief who stealthily takes without the notice of his unsuspecting victim, so my self-esteem was taken. I let the hair under my arms grow and the manicured lines of my eyebrows grew in. The hair on my legs followed suit. I never wore jewelry again; not even my wedding ring. My dark hair fell loosely around my body just above my waist, no style, no added color, just bangs. I looked like a cross between a Native American woman from the 1800s and a feminine version of Grizzly Adams. I barely resembled the woman who had left California.

A thought crossed my mind. I briefly wondered if he could be doing this to make me feel uglier so no one would look at me, to break me, to crush my sense of self. Why couldn't I celebrate what beauty I had been given?

Thanksgiving had passed, ushering in the holiday bustle of Christmas, both of which we no longer celebrated. The winds of winter continued to blow and we were no more sanctified than when we arrived. This town, too, wasn't a place of blessing, so it was time to leave. But not before performing one last good deed.

We met a woman in her early forties who also worked at the hotel in maintenance. She wore her hair pulled back in a ponytail, dressed like a man and could frequently be seen with a lady friend. Scripture condemns homosexuality and Trip therefore dismissed her. She didn't take too kindly to him either, and by virtue of association, she didn't like me, and that bothered me.

We still had the sedan and no need for it. I tried to convince Trip that giving it to this woman would be a good thing. After much deliberation, she became the recipient of the car, our one remaining possession of luxury. Trip quickly changed his tune, seizing the opportunity to make heaven notice the great deed done for the forsaken. "After all, 'when you give to the least of my people, you do unto Me,'" he concluded. I just wanted her to look at me with softness in her eyes.

"While we're chalking up points for heaven," he continued, "We have to let everyone know that we choose God and reject this world and everyone in it. 'If you confess Me before men, I will confess you before my Father.'"

"Yes, but you can't fool God with words. He sees the heart."

Trip didn't even hear my response, still high on his good deed.

He was glad to tell the Morgans where they were 'going'. He grew tired of Mr. Morgan's lack of courage and Mrs. Morgan's constant fawning over him. "Does she really think she's worth noticing?"

Bell didn't escape his ranting either. I thought she should be left alone as Trip had done with the Cunningham's and Dellsworth's before her. She was a true friend to me; maybe that's why he had to do it. Bell, though, was unphased with his accusations that hell was destined for those who followed the way of "savages."

"Trip," she sighed. "You only seek your own interests." She turned to me and said, "Take care of you and come see me when Kuder is sixteen," she laughed. "That means I'll be ninety-six."

Evanston

I jumped from deep sleep to the sound of Kuder's cry, a desperation a mother instinctively hopes she never hears. Darkness lingered at the hotel window. I turned on the light and went to him.

"Mama!" he managed through his sobs. His eyes reached for me, as tears soaked the bed.

I drew him close. "Mama's here. It's okay. I'm here." Kuder was limp. He lay in my arms, sobbing, trying to reciprocate my embrace, but unable to respond.

"Wake up, Trip! Something's wrong with Kuder! He can't move!"

"Wha? What's goin' on?" he asked, rubbing the sleep from his eyes.

Just four months short of his second birthday, Kuder lay paralyzed in a strange bed in a town we had never seen by daylight. We had no one to turn to; we didn't know a soul. We had just left West Yellowstone only days before.

As soon as office hours permitted, we called doctors for help and by noon Kuder was admitted in the hospital, IVs hooked to his tiny hands and a dozen cotton balls taped to the crooks of his arms. I feared for the life of my precious son.

The hospital ran a myriad of tests, but no diagnosis was reached. Their best guess was spinal meningitis. The only other possibility offered was the vaccinations he had received a few days earlier in Idaho.

We managed to continue to see Kuder's pediatrician in Rexburg Idaho where he was born. It was time for his eighteen-month or so check-up and vaccinations when we left West Yellowstone. So, before heading east, we saw Kuder's doctor first.

We were advised to stay in the area to continue Kuder's treatment and monitor his condition. After eight days of sharing Kuder's bed in Wyoming State Hospital, he was discharged. Day by day Kuder regained his motor skills, but, sometimes, I noticed a hint of a tremor in his hands.

The southwest high desert of Wyoming is a desolate place, with scarcely a tree, wind blowing freely without boundaries and few fishing holes, something Trip missed. Kuder still needed treatment, so Evanston became our home. We found an apartment and unloaded the truck, carrying what possessions remained: a futon, pots and pans, his books, the oversized computer chair, Kuder's high chair and our clothes. Our things scarcely filled the place.

"Trip, don't you think we need a few things for the apartment?" I asked.

"Things? Like what?"

"Well, like a table to eat on, a chair for me? I don't have a place to sit, another bed, maybe a dresser?" Trip looked about the apartment, sliding his hands in his pants front pockets, slightly pacing. "You could use the table to study, too?" I added.

"We're supposed to be sojourners."

"I know, just a few things."

In a low grumble he said, "Let's make it quick."

The outing was brief. A Ben Franklin store was closing its doors and selling their fixtures. We bought shelving and brackets for pennies. After much complaining, Trip made a table; it was rickety and crude, but at least it was someplace to put a plate. We then found a beat-up wooden chair, and a queen-size mattress. There was no need for a frame or a box spring, since we could only have that which would fit in the bed of the truck.

"We don't need a dresser. We can put our clothes in piles in the bedroom closets," Trip said.

Trip found temporary work with a construction company. His boss, like most of the men in Montana, Idaho and Wyoming, was a tradesman and if you weren't, you were not part of the club. Although his boss ruthlessly teased him for his lack of practical skills, I sensed the man would have helped him had Trip asked for it. Almost daily, Trip came home frustrated.

"It's my parent's job to prepare me for life and they didn't," he said, kicking the bottom of the bathroom door causing it to shudder as it swung. "I'm a laughing stock at work."

"Maybe you could ask your boss for help?"

"That's a dumb idea. What do you know about men?"

"How else can we learn? You have to start somewhere. We claim to be followers of Christ who should have humility and..."

"Where's your humility talking to me like that?" Trip interrupted.

"I'm just trying to help. Stop blaming and do something about it . . ."

Trip lunged for my neck pressing me up against the kitchen

counter with his hand around my throat. The heat of his breath covered my face.

"Watch it, Cubby," he said.

Time stopped. We stood nose-to-nose for a long moment. In his eyes, I couldn't help but notice the storm mounting. What was coming? His hold wasn't life threatening I told myself, yet a primal fear was warning me. He had never touched me before with such aggression.

I lowered my eyes then reached for his hand and released myself from his grip. Without a word and without a glance, I walked away. I found Kuder playing in the living room and sat down hard.

'If a man says he comes in My name and he has not love, he is a false prophet.' If you have not love, you have not truth.' These scriptures raced through my mind. Trip spent the life we shared studying these sacred writings and it seemed he only internalized passages that supported his convenience. But I didn't dare bring these discrepancies to his attention. I began to wonder about my fate and that of my son, if I spoke without discretion.

Winter came again. We had lived in Evanston for just over a year following the same pattern as before. No friends, no involvement, no permanence. Yet in a way, we had more connection with the community in Evanston than in any other place. The hospital staff and doctors knew us and that made me feel safe, but Trip was uncomfortable. Kuder no longer needed monitoring although the doctors advised that we stay close. But it was time to leave again.

"It's time to find a place with more outdoor recreation—a place where God, nature and fishing coexist," Trip announced.

In reality, he needed to take me away from the place where he was the one being monitored.

I felt more alone now and less close to Trip, yet my maternal clock tugged at my heart. I wanted a playmate for Kuder. I wanted a second son, or maybe I wanted more of Trip that I could only get through his seed. Although sex happened less and less after the vasectomy incident, we left Evanston in April carrying in my womb his second son.

Cody

I don't know if Cody, Wyoming, had more fishing, but the rodeo capital of the world is where we landed. We found a two-bedroom apartment on the outskirts of town near a public playground and irrigation canal. The dwelling resembled an elongated box; the cage that would become my home.

We entered the living room, which passed through the kitchen, by the bathroom into two small bedrooms in the back, one to the left and the other straight ahead. Our possessions hardly filled the apartment.

Kuder was three now and very much aware of playmates. We took him to the nearby park to get out, and as he played, Trip continued his sermons. Trip wouldn't allow Kuder to play with other children and told him repeatedly, "Those kids will teach you bad habits and drag you into the world. All you need is us."

Kuder looked at them wanting to play. My heart felt heavy, as I understood my son's longing. I, too, yearned to be a part of life. Main Street in Cody bustled with gatherings, warm smiles and an inviting western atmosphere. I longed to be invited, to live a life, not constant flux. But I reminded myself that the separation from others was necessary to find truth, and that its revelation had to be within reach. But I couldn't deny that the path was becoming more than I could bear.

I took Kuder's hands and knelt to his level.

"Let's go to the canal and play in the water. We can make boats from the leaves and twigs and race them. How does that sound?" Kuder's eyes brightened. "Hey, I saw some wood planks near the water. Maybe we can make a bridge to the other side. I saw some trees. We could climb them, too."

Trip offered nothing.

"Yeah!" Kuder blurted as he jumped up and down. The three of us headed back toward the apartment, first stopping by the canal. Trip excused himself to study and left us alone. Kuder and I spent many afternoons at the canal as another option to an occupied park.

Trip found a temporary job working nights at a water plant about thirty miles out of town. While he slept during the day, Kuder and I scarcely filled our days, stretching meal times, taking walks to nowhere and occupying ourselves outside, searching for diversion yet unable to mask our reality. Although the hope in Kuder's eyes never dimmed, my light was waning. The woman who once couldn't keep from beaming, could now barely smile.

"Mama, can we drive somewhere?" Kuder asked.

"Daddy drives, Mi'jo. Let's wait for him to take us."

Kuder looked at me for a long while. As I contemplated my son's stare, I realized that I had lost my fight. I sealed my fate to stay with Trip when I resolved not to leave him. In public, I made sure to support my husband, but I resisted him at home. Now, I no longer fought against him, but fought to defend him. After all, I could always find a path to see things his way.

All summer we spent the hottest part of the day inside the apartment made dark by draped blankets on windows. Now the queen-sized mattress rested on the living room floor where Kuder napped and where Kuder and I slept. The back two rooms were Trip's. There, he slept on the futon during the day and studied when he wasn't at work.

I sat alone in a dark apartment as Kuder napped and Trip slept. Sounds of children laughing and adults talking as they walked by outside intensified the harsh futility of my existence. All I could do was sit. No TV, no radio, no reading, other than the Bible but that was becoming tiresome. No hobbies, no friends, no one with whom to share a trivial conversation. I missed Bell, my friend.

I worked on being a great cook and keeping a nice home, but even those chores were chastised. Trip's words echoed in my mind.

"Why do you occupy yourself with mundane worldly tasks when you should be seeking the kingdom of God?"

"I think it's important to eat healthy and provide a warm atmosphere for our home."

"I thought you were a spiritual woman. I thought you wanted more than what everyone else wants."

That rebuke also became tiresome.

Kuder awoke from his nap and wanted to play. His excitement disturbed Trip.

"Cubby, keep the noise down! I'm trying to get some sleep."

Desperation grew inside of me. All the blessed day Kuder and I were trapped. How many times could we go downtown, to the park, to the canal without an acquaintance to change it up once in a while? Or even his company? Physically, I grew tired.

I was diagnosed with hypothyroidism during my fifth month of pregnancy. Even breathing became too much to bear. Trip was unsympathetic.

"You wanted a second child so you got what you deserve."

Although I did want another baby and perhaps the pregnancy brought on the condition, I wanted another boy. Kuder would have a playmate and he wouldn't be alone like me.

The thyroid treatment brought me back to life and I could again deal with the heavy load we carried. But the medication was not enough to mask my ever-growing despair.

"Everything in this life is a distraction," Trip announced, coming out of the room into the kitchen. I was startled. I thought he was asleep.

"A job, family, friends, holidays, material things, nature and even food are all deterrents to finding the next life," he continued.

I was so raw, so stripped of my natural defense mechanisms, that I could do nothing but feel the complete ramifications of his newly unearthed doctrine.

"Then why live?!" I whispered. Trip ignored me.

Everything he mentioned was life! We all want that perfect career or family; to share our material possessions with friends and loved ones during the holidays or find rejuvenation in nature or pleasure in food to lighten our load. *Then, what's the point?!* I was screaming inside, but all I managed to say was, "Wow," as I slumped down into the chair, utterly deflated.

Unfazed by my state of depletion, Trip continued to say, "Cubby, I can't take the birth of another child. We can make the journey with one child, but not another. What if we give the baby up for adoption when he is born?"

My heart could take no more. Tears streamed down my lifeless face. *How many blows could this man give me?! How much more could I take before he took my life?* We were spiraling down deep into a pit of doubtful return. *I can't do this anymore!* I thought. My bowels ached. I wanted to die right then and there, but the thought of Kuder and my son within pulled me back to fight.

Trip was not going to take my son! How could he ask a mother to do such a thing?

I had only a couple months to convince my husband that the treasure within my womb was a blessing and we could be a family on this elusive path for truth. I looked at Trip through my tears and managed to say, "We don't have to decide anything right now."

I mustered the strength to rise and looked around, then called for Kuder. "I'm gonna take him to the park."

I watched Trip retreat to one of the back rooms and shut the door with not so much as a glance at us.

The next two months passed with barely a conversation about adoption. Both of us seemed to avoid the topic. I knew why I shunned the idea yet it didn't occur to me as to why Trip hadn't pursued the issue. I felt somewhat safe if we didn't speak of it, as if we never had the conversation in the first place, yet I was constantly haunted by the thought.

Two o'clock in the morning of November 18, my labor pains were increasingly strong. Trip drove me to the hospital a few miles on the other side of town. It was seventeen below zero that morning. A thin layer of white powder covered the already frozen streets.

The nurse examined the progress of my labor. "You're dilated two centimeters," she said. "You'll need to stay and register."

The baby is coming! Apprehension came over me.

"Miss, miss, are you okay with that?" The nurse repeated.

"Uh … yes, that's fine."

I was glad the nurse said I had to stay. I didn't want to go home to labor with my husband. I would find more support here.

"Hey Cubby, I'm going home to sleep. I'm tired. I'll be back in a few hours."

I sat up and leaned forward ready to reach for his hand to ask him to stay, but resigned not to react. What was I thinking? I don't want him here. "All right," I said and watched him walk out the door.

Trip returned after breakfast. I had made little progress in dilation. Part of me was hesitant to have the child. I feared how Trip might take him away from me. *My baby is another gift to me from the man I love. How could I part with such a prize?* I anguished with the thought.

Labor took its time. Seventeen hours later, through back labor and no medication, my son was born. A beautiful twenty-two-and-a-half inch, ten-pound, eleven-ounce boy lay on my belly and suckled. He was solid; a muscularly defined infant who already held up his head. The hospital staff referred to him as a "tank."

"Your son gets the biggest baby of the year award," The doctor said, showing me a collage of baby footprints born in that hospital that year. "Look at the size of that footprint!" He boasted.

That's how he got the nickname "Tank."

Trip feigned tears of joy. "I have another son!" he managed.

I knew Trip enough to recognize he could deliver what his expectant audience awaited. I understood what no one else knew.

We brought Tank home to a sad retreat. My heart ached with the thought of parting with him. *What's going to happen? Is he going to yank him from my arms? How will I stop him? My son!* My timidity turned into resolve. *No Trip! You will not succeed! You will never take my son!* I did what I could to endear Tank to Trip.

"Don't you think Tank got your grandpa's genes? He's built just like him. Solid."

Trip looked at the baby. "Yeah, you're right. He's quite a little man. He reminds me a lot of Grampa." Then a slight smirk drew across his lips.

He never spoke of adoption again, but not because he became endeared to the boy; rather, he already had another plan.

Hell

"I quit my job at the water plant."

Thank God! Internally I gave a sigh of relief. How I hated the prison of a life we led while he worked nights. Maybe now we could spend some time together. "But, why?" I asked without missing a beat.

"Even my job is keeping me from finding truth. I think we're close." He looked around, running his hands back through his hair, his blue eyes wide. "I just have to keep studying."

"What do you need me to do?"

"You need to pray and pray hard." With that he retreated into the bedroom to study and shut the door, the echo of the slam still lingering in the apartment.

He didn't work nights anymore, but now he studied scriptures almost twenty-four hours a day! He barely ate, he barely slept and we spent very little time together. Kuder, Tank and I were very much alone and the weight of that fell brutally on me. I recalled my companion, the pain that joined me when I said goodbye to my family. My burden never left me; it only grew heavier.

I set Kuder beside me to play with his few second-hand toys I managed to get for him and placed Tank in his car seat at arm's distance. Never before in my life, nor ever again have I prayed so fervently. I asked for humility. I begged for the one attribute I thought would always keep us safe and in check.

"Cubby," I heard Trip say from the darkened hallway. A few seconds later he appeared in the kitchen.

"I'm here."

"I feel like something's not connecting in my brain; like the neurons from one side aren't making it to the other side."

For some reason I responded in a matter-of-fact sort of way to his distress. "Honestly Trip, you can't have a blow to the head and everything be normal."

Twenty-nine years before, when he was five years old, Trip was in a car accident. Unrestrained, he flew from the back seat and came to a halt with the meeting of his head on the dashboard when the car impacted a tree. One eighth of his skull at the hairline, above his left eye was replaced with a metal plate. Nearly the entire year of Kindergarten, he wore a turban. After a year of surgeries and hospital visits, his family was happy he had made a complete recovery. They could move on, putting the accident behind them.

Trip stared off into space. That accident always seemed to be in the back of his mind. Maybe I shouldn't have brought it up, or had more compassion. But I didn't. I changed the subject. "You must be hungry. Can I get you something to eat?"

"Sure," he said now looking down.

"Will you stay with us?"

Trip took a seat in his oversized computer chair at our makeshift table, exhausted and beaten. I quickly put something together and set it before him taking a seat on the beat-up chair, sensing he wanted to talk.

"Cubby, we don't have to give up the baby for adoption. I think it's me who needs to leave."

Liberation and shock flooded into my soul. I was relieved that Trip wanted to leave and overjoyed that it was not Tank who had to go, yet surprised that I would instinctively react this way because I loved Trip still. Up until this moment, going our separate ways never seemed possible; even in West Yellowstone when I made plans to leave him, a divorce always seemed beyond the walls of my existence. The cage I lived in began to crumble and the rays of freedom began spilling into it. It felt so good. I could taste a life with just my two boys and me.

"What? What are you saying?"

"I made a vow that I'd never marry. Way before I met you I made this promise. Maybe that's why I'm not getting any answers. Maybe you should go home to your family."

"What vow? Why hadn't you mentioned this before? What do you really mean to say? Is this an excuse?" It was as if he wasn't even listening to me. He didn't respond.

I studied his face. I saw a man I didn't recognize, emotionally disconnected from us and in anguish; a different pain than what I was experiencing.

He rose from the table without touching his food and without a word, returned to study.

An hour passed and I dared to knock on the door to bring him something to eat.

"Trip? Can I come in? I have some food for you." No answer. I turned the door knob and gently pushed the door ajar.

"Trip? Are you alright?"

Still no answer. My heart began to pound. I continued to

push open the door. Sitting underneath the window, as if left for dead after a fight in a back alley, sat my husband. His head hung to one side; one leg bent, the other sprawled out. His lifeless arms hung at his side and his eyes wide open and vacant. I dropped the food and ran to him, grabbing his shoulders, shaking him.

"Trip! Trip!"

He said nothing. Then, the seemingly lifeless body responded to me. He lifted his head and rolled his vulnerable blue eyes to meet mine.

"Cubby, I saw myself."

"What do you mean, 'saw yourself'?"

"I'm a man full of pride. I'm a disgusting creature thinking my intellect could outwit God and con answers from Him."

I sat back on my heels in awe of his humility. I took a breath and slowly released it as my body, taking over, took a moment to relax. Was this his breaking point? Maybe he could turn to God for forgiveness, no more fighting, no more anger and maybe there could be peace. Maybe my prayers for humility were answered. I spoke softly and offered. "God is forgiving, Trip."

"Yeah, maybe," he said, looking down, away from me. We sat silent for a long minute. "Can I be alone?" he finally asked.

I kissed his cheek and touched his hand as I rose to leave and closed the door behind me. Immediately, I found Kuder, took his hand and went to Tank, sitting in his infant swing. There, I fell to the floor to pray for my husband.

"Mama, you okay?" Kuder asked.

"Yes Mi'jo, let's pray for Daddy."

"Tank?"

"Yes, he seems to be all right in the baby swing. Can you wind it up some more?"

Kuder smiled and eagerly turned the crank to give his baby brother a little more swing time and then came and sat with me. I reached my arm around Kuder and brought him under me like a hen that corralls her chicks, hopeful our life was going to change for the better.

Trip burst from the back bedroom. He made his way down the hallway, stumbling over nothing as he braced himself on the wall. The raging sea now warred in his eyes.

"Cubby, do you see that?" He demanded, looking here and there. "I can't stay here any longer! God is going to strike me down!"

I got up, holding Kuder's hand as he was half asleep. "See what? What are you talking about?"

"The ugly demons!"

I stood upright as if being interrogated. A black blanket of fear came down as if someone had just thrown it onto me.

"They're everywhere! They keep encircling me!"

The apartment fell ominously dark and heavy.

I looked around with eyes as wide as the sun. I didn't see anything, but I felt a wanton presence. A haze of dreadful grays consumed the atmosphere, as if something like smoke oozed in. The air became difficult to breathe. As Dracula envelopes his victim praying down upon her to suck her blood, so horror enclosed me, numbing my nerve to react.

I searched the apartment, looking for my husband. A pitiful sight wrenched my insides. I knew I was alone. The man I looked to for everything could not be reached, lost in a war

I could not see. For the first time, I feared for my life and the lives of my sons. *My boys!* I reacted.

"Tank's asleep now. Let me take him from the swing and lay him down in the back bedroom." I directed to Trip who paced the kitchen floor, unconcerned with anyone, ready to lash out at anything. "Kuder, go play in the living room, okay, Mi'jo?"

I ran with Tank tucked safely in my arms to place him in the back bedroom and sprinted back to stand in the kitchen, a protective distance between Trip and my two sons.

"They're after me! I can't stay here anymore! God is going to kill me for breaking my vow to Him, for my pride and the stock I've put into my studies." He turned to me like a defensive snake, ready to strike. "You're not safe either. You can't go home to your family." his voice becoming more gruff. "We left them, remember?"

I was involuntarily shaking now. Somehow I found the courage to reach within for my few fragments of strength that remained to calm my husband. My commitment to him compelled me. "W-W-Wait, sit, let me make you some tea. It, it will calm your nerves."

He sat at our makeshift table in the oversized computer chair. I brought him his tea and sat opposite him in the beat-up wooden chair.

I fought to keep my composure and finally said, "Trip, you're going to be alright. Just ask for forgiveness. God knows we make mistakes." My eyes reached for my husband, pleading for him to come back to me from his darkness. "I know it is difficult. Think about the boys; about us. Don't you think God would want you to take responsibility for having a family and forget your promise of the past?" I took another breath. "God doesn't need us. We need Him and He has already pardoned you for our sake. He loves us!"

What seemed like forever passed between us as a familiar man appeared. The raging seas in his eyes seemed to calm. He was no longer pressed in a panic. The cool pools of water were soothing to look at again. He reached for me and took my wrist. He held it tight, rubbing his thumb on the top side of my hand as if he had something desperate to say to me. Only silence fell. We looked into each other's eyes and I could swear that a hint of mist clouded the pools of water.

"Thank you for the tea," he managed.

"You're welcome," I whispered.

Thank you God! We're going to come out of this! I thought. Hope grew in my belly, thankful that I had given my husband the remaining fragments of my being. I had nothing more he could take.

He looked down at our hands laced together then touched them with his other hand. Staring at them, he gradually let go. He rose from the table and turned away from me, his head tilted down, gazing at the floor, hands in his pockets. He seemed to be moving something with this foot as if in deep thought. He started to turn back around to me. I anticipated open arms. As he turned, I was horrified. The caged lion was back! The violent seas in his eyes could not be contained any longer. He looked to and fro ready to run.

"I have to go. I can't stay here," he said as he pushed by me toward the door. I jumped from my seat and pressed myself against the wall. After he passed, I ran to Kuder playing in the living room and put my trembling arms around him. *Thank God*

Tank was asleep in the back room. My stomach ached as it churned in knots. Trip was going down a path I could no longer follow.

He turned back around to me as I held Kuder tightly in my arms. The storm in his eyes raging. He took a long look at us, but not as though taking a mental picture of the family, rather planning his next move. He ran toward the back bedroom. No! *Where is he going? Is he going to take Tank with him! No! God no!*

I let go of Kuder and put him behind me and watched Trip, ready to pounce if he went into the room where Tank slept. He didn't! A few seconds later, Trip ran back with a sports bag. *Filled with his belongings?* I thought. And he lunged toward the front door. He turned the knob, pulled the door open and then looked back at me.

"Call your family. Go home. Your brothers will take care of you." And with that he turned and walked out into the night.

That was the last time I ever saw him.

A warm presence entered the room pushing out the darkness. "It is finished. You are free," I felt it say.

Alone

Kuder ran to the large living room window looking out into the dark night sky. Snow fell as if trying to brighten the darkness we both felt in our souls. He stared as his father drove away in the half-ton truck. I stared too, not having moved from the place I stood when Trip walked out the door. I watched the truck become a blur as the snow devoured it; only the brake lights were visible.

"Mama," I felt my son's tiny hand wrap around mine, not noticing he was no longer at the window. Lowering my head, our eyes locked. "I'm glad Daddy left. I don't want him here anymore." I was looking at my three-year-old, while listening to the words of a man.

I knelt down and took my son in my arms. I gave a sigh of relief. The blackness that was just here left with the parting of my husband. *Tank!* "We have to check on Tank."

"Okay, Mama."

Together, we brought Tank to the front room and together we lay on the queen-sized mattress. With one son under each arm, I held my treasure overwhelmed with the boundless love I had for them and the sorrow of the loss of my husband.

I jumped to the sound of the phone ringing. I didn't realize we had fallen asleep. It was Trip.

"Cubby, I made a mistake. I shouldn't have left you. Things are getting worse."

How I wanted to drop the phone. The blackness reached through the phone. "What do you mean?"

"The demons are all around me, but now they're leaving marks on my skin."

I couldn't say anything. I didn't want him back. All I wanted was to hang up.

"I drove all night. I have to do something! I gotta go!" The dial tone sounded. I threw the receiver as if I had picked up a log loaded with spiders.

I looked at the boys now squirming on the bed. *I need to nurse Tank. Kuder must be starving.* It had been a while since we'd eaten, but I wasn't at all hungry. I forced myself to eat for the sake of Tank.

A few hours passed. The phone rang again.

"Cubby, I'm in hospital."

"What!?"

"I went to the emergency room for the doctor to cut out my right eye. You know the verse. 'If your right eye offends you; cut it from you.'"

"What are you saying!?"

"I use my eyes to study and therefore I have been offending God. That's why I haven't found any answers. I've been thinking that my studies would bring me to God instead of God leading me to Himself. And now they think I'm crazy."

"I . . . Trip . . ."

"I have to go."

Days passed without word from Trip. I spent my waking hours shut in a lonely apartment. We barely went outside. I was too tired to move. I didn't know what to do. I barely ate. If it weren't for my sons, I wouldn't have taken a bite. No one knew of the tragedy happening in our little apartment. No one visited. No one helped. Even now, I thought I'd get struck by the wrath of God somehow. I still feared hell would consume me even without my husband.

A ring sounded from the object I dreaded to bring to my ear. Would it be Trip telling me of more demons? Would I feel the tentacles of darkness reach for me through the phone?

"H-Hello?" I managed.

"Hello, Mrs. Donovich?" the cool voice on the other end echoed.

"Y-Y-Yes?"

"Trip shot his right eye out with a pellet gun. By the time some kind of care got to him, it was unable to be saved. It will have to be replaced with a glass eye . . ."

The phone slid from my ear, out of my hand and onto the floor.

Abandoned

I fell to my knees again. I prayed to Jesus, the son of God, through whom all things came to be and through whom we received all things and begged for help.

I begged to understand how the man I always dreamed of marrying could turn out so wrong? I begged to understand why, if I loved this man with all my soul, unselfishly giving of myself even before myself, would he not love me, but instead abandon me? Why did I trade my precious family for a truth that never came? Why would he allow people to use religion to deceive? Why was my own husband allowed to use God to deceive me?!

A presence came into the room, the same warmth that replaced the darkness the night Trip left. Was this Jesus? But this was not the Jesus who ejected the Pharisees who traded in the temple. He was an insecure fellow. Compassionate, yes, but unforthcoming. He sat crouched on the window sill.

"Listen honey, I can't help you with this one. This is out of my league."

And with that, like every man for himself, the presence leapt out the window.

Crash! A sledgehammer slammed into my heart, shattering it into a billion pieces. I physically buckled over then onto the floor. The foundation of my life no longer existed.

I believed that family ties can never be broken, yet I broke my ties with them as I broke their hearts. My husband was supposed to love me. Why else would he ask me to marry him? But he never really did. A good wife supports her husband and look where it has taken me! Marriage is forever, yet my husband abandoned me. God never tests beyond what you're able to withstand, even though here I lay on the floor, destroyed. People, who flock under the shelter of religion, don't deceive, but like a teenage virgin raped and assaulted, I was left profoundly violated. Jesus is supposed to be my mediator to God and, alas, He too, has deserted me.

In that instant, what seemed like a veil was lifted, opened for me to see our present reality. I stopped thinking and brought myself to half-way sitting. I saw everything so clearly. Everything seemed like a play, well acted out and convincing, but still entertainment, a distraction from reality. It was a lot to see. And even more difficult to grasp.

Society. This pressure from "the norm" that society has set up to follow its lead. Where did that come from? This norm spreads in all media, schooling, even culture. Who created this "norm?" Who is behind society? Are they one and the same?

Religion. A game of guilt to follow some arbitrary rules to all be the same. If you follow its teachings, you are holy. If not, you are a sinner. Whose interpretation is this?

Education. To educate is to enlighten. But there's a debonair snake withering among this beautiful idea of enlightenment that with an education you will have a better life, not necessarily become enlightened, but a better life. Is a better life guaranteed though? At what cost, when individuality is frowned upon?

In my culture, or at least how I grew up, women had a curfew, but men did not. Men did not have to clean. Women did. A woman's voice is not as heard as a man's. Men could sleep around. Women were whores if they did. My culture is not who I am, but rather how I was brought into society. And whose society?

Everything is a lie! But what was not a lie then? What was there to believe in? Why was I shown this? What am I supposed to do with this? I don't understand! Upon what then, do I lay the foundation of my life when the foundation that I had known, disintegrated with the force of pushing the boundaries of life? How am I supposed to live when all that I once believed has been revealed to be faulty at best?

Why was I shown this? This revelation was far worse than all the suffering from leaving my family, Trip not accepting me and my boys, and all of the unimaginable anguish of our journey. A person can lose many parts of their life and still continue, but how does one live when belief in everything is taken? Upon what does one build a life?

Can dust ever be reassembled?

Home

The phone rang again. This time I was making the call.

"Elo?"

"Dad?"

"*¿Mija? Eres tú?*" My daughter? Is it you?

"*Si, Papá.*"

My Dad dropped the phone, which was picked up by my mother who, knew it was me, as my Dad ran outside and fell to his knees thanking his God that his most sensitive child was alive.

He told me later, "I asked my God every chance I got to keep you safe and that you would call. When you did I could not give thanks within the confines of a man-made structure. I had to go out into His creation and thank Him for answering my prayer."

Twenty-four hours later, my Mom, Dad and sister, the very one who wouldn't speak to me before I left six years ago, were in my apartment. Finally I could share my sons with my family.

"Would you like to return home with us?" my mother asked, sensing the delicate situation.

I vacillated between wanting to return to the family I so loved and fearing that I would be struck by a lightning bolt the minute I left the apartment. "*We left our families, remember?*" Trip's voice echoed, warning.

"Just do it already!" my sister said growing impatient with my indecision.

I loaded my cast iron pans, the same ones I use to this day, with our few clothes and we boarded a small two engine plane to Salt Lake City.

The engines started up with a roar. *You're going to Hell for returning to your family,* Trip's voice warned. My eyes were still wide as the sun, not having taken their normal shape since the night of the demons. In that instance a presence appeared. It was dark and somber, yet love was there. It said nothing. Was it the same presence that came in after Trip left? Was it the same presence that leaped out the window? Was this death coming for me? I thought for sure this was the end of my life. *At least my sons are with me.* The plane violently snarled through the sky. *The plane's gonna explode! How can I escape?* There was no escape. With no other option, I resigned myself. *God, if you're going to strike me down, there's no where I can hide. Here I am. Do what You will.*

The aircraft never exploded. The loving yet somber presence disappeared, and my precious sons and I made it back to California, back to the Gold Country where I grew up, to the only home I had ever really known.

PART III

Rebuilding
Dust

My boys and I had nothing, nor was I in any condition to be
on my own so we lived with my parents. I was so happy
to live with my mom and dad again; to share my boys with my
unconditionally loving parents. I had thought that I would never
get this opportunity. I was still catatonic, however. *"You're going to
hell for going back to your family."* Trip's words would still echo in
my mind. It was a confusing time. I would go between moments
of complete gratitude and moments of complete fear.

I found my father working outside in the garden, tending
his vegetables and fruit trees. Almost daily, I went to him. I had
been brainwashed. That much I knew. And I also knew that it
was my upbringing that both kept me sane while living with
Trip and also led me toward him. But I had forgotten so many
of the good lessons of my youth.

"Dad, remind me how you taught us to think," I'd ask as I
sat down beside him. "Sometimes I think I'm going to go crazy."

"You can if you want," he responded, not lifting his head from
braiding the garlic he had harvested. His cool response brought
security and clarity. I didn't feel afraid or out of control. *I can
do this*, I thought.

"De demonio, de santo, de loco, todos tenemos un poco. We all have a little demon, saint and crazy in us," he continued. "What part of you do you want to grow? The choice is yours."

The fact that I never scared my father with any question or situation brought me great comfort and stability. I gave my dad a hug and got up and went about my day.

A couple days later, there I was again with my dad, asking the same question.

"Dad, remind me of how you taught us to think again."

"Mija, I don't like repeating myself. One time is all you need to hear," he said.

"I know Dad, but I need you to tell me again," I insisted.

Calmly, he repeated what he told me just days before. This went on for nearly eighteen months. The conversations changed a bit each time and each time a little more understanding was recaptured.

Later, when I was able to be on my own, our talks continued. My dad would come over unannounced and find a seat at the kitchen table. The kitchen was the heart of our Latin home growing up and continues to be in mine as well. He always asked if I had any Mexican chocolate and if I could fix him a cup. Of course I would. It made me happy, so I made sure to always have some. I enjoyed our special times when he came just to see me.

"Mi'ja, I'm sorry. I'm sorry I didn't teach you how to build fences, change electrical wires, and plumbing. I thought your husband would take care of these needs for you, for your home." He said with tears in his eyes. "Now, you are by yourself. I never thought I'd see this. But I will help you and teach your boys everything I can while I am able and on this earth." My dad was a traditional man from the old country, flawed for sure, but rich in character.

Kuder and I both saw therapists for years after leaving the hell we lived through with Trip. Many nights Kuder would be so angry. Most of the time he was angry, not really knowing why. I knew why.

"Mama, will I act or end up like my dad?"

"That is certainly a possibility," I said. "You have a choice, Mi'jo. You can either respond how your father did or you can choose to respond how you want. There are always two ways to look at a situation. One makes us feel bad. The other makes us feel good." A moment of silence cradled us as we contemplated the words. Breaking the silence I asked,

"How do you want to respond?"

"I don't want to be like my dad."

"You don't have to be. That's the beautiful thing. You have a choice. Every time you feel angry or that there is no other way to be but mean, remember, the choice of which path to take is yours. Find the path that makes you feel good about your actions and do that."

We looked into each other's eyes. I could see that he understood, and the demeanor of his body changed from tension to ease. This beautiful, innocent child always chose the higher road. It was admirable and remarkable. He was only five years old.

I stayed with him, helping him process his emotions until he had some peace and then I'd let him fall asleep. Like me, constantly asking my father for clarity, Kuder and I went through this almost nightly process for about the same amount of time as my father and I had done.

Divorce

My brothers suggested that it would be in my best interest to separate myself from Trip legally, because if he ended up hurting someone or something, I would be liable. Divorce seemed way too harsh. I still deeply cared for this man, yet I knew our life together was no more. There was no chance I could ever again trust our safety in that union. It was as if he died. I lost my husband, my life with this man, and any hope of any future with him. There would be no watching our sons play sports, having girlfriends or growing old together. It was just me and my two little boys now with nothing to our name.

No one around me saw it that way, though. I didn't receive any, "I'm sorry for your loss." Instead, I felt my family say, "Well, you made the choices to do what you did. Here are your consequences." Or maybe what I was sensing was the conditioning of Trip's callous behavior. Either way, no one ever said, "Hey, it sucks what you went through," or anything of that nature.

I was prompted to go on welfare since I had nothing and no way to support myself. That felt horrible. I felt small, embarrassed, unsupported and ashamed. At the same time, I understood my family's reaction. I knew what choices I had made and I didn't make them lightly. I was prepared to pay any recompense that my family saw fit for me to pay. I never wanted to hurt them, but I did. My actions seemed like a slap in the face to my family. They surely did not convey how much I loved and appreciated them, how we grew up and all the love we had for one another. I felt truly blessed to be a part of my family, but something pulled me to take this road to find this elusive idea of "truth." I didn't expect them to understand, but it still hurt.

Legal separation felt like less of a blow.

White and majestic stood the 1913 county courthouse. I walked up to the grand entrance into this magnificent structure of our small gold rush town. My lawyer was by my side. We sat in a beautiful hardwood courtroom waiting to be seen by the judge. It was our turn.

"Your Honor, my name is Elizabeth so and so. I am representing this woman and her two sons. We are asking for a legal separation and sole physical and legal custody of the minor boys from this union."

"How old are the boys?"

"One and four, Your Honor."

"How does the defendant plead?"

"No response has been filed, sir."

"Why do you ask for sole physical and legal custody?"

"Well Your Honor, the father of these two boys shot his eyes out with a pellet gun for religious reasons. We are seeking the legal and physical protection of this woman and her children"

The judge's mouth fell open and his gavel hit the sound box. "Granted."

Final
Phone Call

"You're a liar! You're not a holy man! You didn't want to honor God! You didn't say goodbye to find truth! You left because you were too afraid to face life because you knew you were weak, but you wanted to seem strong with your religious mumbo jumbo. Your insecurity led you to use God to make yourself seem mighty."

"You were embarrassed because my brothers and sister and mom and dad are stronger than you and we are an immigrant family! English was our second language and yet we have overcome and accomplished more than you! You wanted to take me away from my family, knowing that they would have defended me and questioned YOU!"

"You are manipulative! And you're clever. You know that I am a genuine woman. You used religion and my faith to try to make me weak, to make me less, to make me submit to your warped perception of love."

"What about the verse that says, 'Husbands, love your wives, just as Christ loved the church and gave himself up for her?' *NIV Ephesians 5:25* Husbands are to love their wives FIRST!

You always demanded that I was to love YOU, NO MATTER WHAT! NO MATTER HOW WRONG YOU WERE! What about you?!" I caught myself yelling and then stopped.

Silence.

No rebuttal came from Trip. That was strange. He always had a fight in him, but not this time, just silence.

"I'm not going to hell." I broke the silence. "You need to worry about yourself."

"You should be ashamed! You only thought of your own well-being. The honor that you should have had in being my husband and the father of my boys, you threw away. You lost the best people that ever happened to you!"

"I'm so mad at you!! I loved you with all my being! Few people are lucky to be loved like that. But you were too blind to see." I took a breath. Silence filled the space. Then I whispered.

"I loved you . . . I love you still."

These were the last words I ever spoke to Trip. I left no words unsaid. I don't know if my accusations were accurate, I just knew that my words came from the deep-seated pain of loss and betrayal. It was over. But, like the last soldier left standing in a field after a devastating battle surrounded by death and destruction, I put down my sword, a look of 'why?' on my face and stumbled away. I was not a victor that day, just a woman who knew that there was nothing I could do other than to walk away from the man I loved to try to rebuild my life that had been shattered.

I had gone to hell with Trip and now I said to hell with him and to all that I once believed.

I changed my papers from legal separation to divorce.

Trip

Trip continued down that path the night he left; the path that I could not follow. He proceeded to blow out his other eye. This one they could save but even still, he is now legally blind. He later ran away from his parents' home, a mental ward, the judge. I don't know exactly from whom or what, but during his escape he ran across a freeway and was hit by a truck. Many bones were broken all over his body. It was a miracle that he did not die. For a couple of years after, he vacillated between bouts in mental institutions and his parents' home. Where he is now and what has happened, I do not know.

I couldn't save him!!! . . . I couldn't save him . . .

He was, and is, the only one who could.

The Ring

Her eyes were full of compassion and embarrassment. Trip's mom was in my house, the home where my brothers and sister and I grew up. It was by no means the plush surroundings that she was used to. At this point, I was done with feeling less for being me. As it was, I had, by far, more blessings than she could ever understand. So, I made her come and stay at my family home. She tried her best to conceal her awkwardness. To her credit, she was gracious and she genuinely enjoyed visiting and playing with the boys. Afterall, Kuder looked so much like her son.

I asked her to follow me to the back bedroom where Tank, Kuder and I slept. I turned to her once she was in the room and reached out my hand.

"Here" I said, reaching my closed fist to her holding a small object. She looked down and I opened my hand. It was my wedding ring. She took it. She examined it without raising her head. She knew it well. The center diamond was a family heirloom. After a moment, she looked up. Once our eyes met, I said. "The symbol for what this ring once stood no longer exists. I know what that diamond means to you. You should have it back."

She didn't say a word, yet understanding, regret and gratitude filled her eyes.

Back
to School

I returned to school to get my teaching credential when Tank was nine months old. I had been preparing the boys for what I was about to do. Kuder seemed to understand and was happy to see me getting stronger. Tank was still so young. I picked them both up and squeezed the precious lives I had in my arms. I released our embrace, placing Kuder on the ground and got down on his level. I put Tank to one side of my lap, my arm holding him firmly against my body. And then I pulled Kuder close.

"Mama is going back to school now so I can make a home for us, okay?"

"Okay, mama," Kuder said with a smile.

"Gramma and Grampa will be with you and take care of you and Tank while I'm gone. Take care of your brother, okay?" I said as I kissed Kuder's cheek and squeezed him again with one arm.

"Okay, mama," he said tenderly.

I turned to Tank. "Gramma and Grampa will take care of you while I'm gone, okay? I'll be right back," I said, kissing his face.

I got up, readjusting Tank on my hip with one arm while

holding on to Kuder's hand with my other hand. I walked to my mother and put Tank in her arms. My father came beside my mom as I put Kuder's hand in my father's hand.

"*Yo te los cuido mija. No te preocupes.* I'll take care of them. Don't worry," my mother said, feeling my pain of leaving my boys. My mother was an extraordinary woman, poised, feminine, silenced by her culture, but a resilient warrior by nature. She loved relentlessly, beared all without complaint, yet spoke her mind poignantly.

I got in the car. I smiled and waved as my mother held Tank and as my father held Kuder's hand in his. They all waved. Kuder looked happy. Tank looked confused. *Where is mama going?* My boys had spent every hour of every day of their lives with me until this moment. I started the car and pulled out of the driveway. Slowly, they disappeared in the rearview mirror. Once out of sight, tears streamed down my face. I couldn't see. I turned the corner, pulled over, and sobbed. My heart felt like it was about to explode. Simultaneously, I felt such pain and such love. It hurt me so much to leave my boys. All I wanted was to be with them. I felt so much love in my heart for them and such love and gratitude for my parents.

The day had come. My first day of class. I went to the teacher boxes to pick up my materials for the first day of school as I was instructed to do. I saw my name on my teacher box in the high school office. A wave of pride and accomplishment came over me. I don't know if I was smiling, but it felt like I was, ear to ear. I did it! I was a professional. I had come back to life. No one knew of the hell from which I had come. To everyone else, I was just another young, first-year teacher eager to meet her students. I never spoke of my life with Trip, either. If people asked, I stretched the truth. "My husband died in a car accident when my baby was six weeks old." That pretty much ended the conversation. Afterall, that is how old Tank was when Trip walked out the door. And Trip had been in a car accident when he was five years old that changed his life forever. It was so much easier to tell this lie than to tell the truth. The truth was so strange and made for a way too long explanation that most people didn't have time, nor did they care.

Life was good and I was grateful. I felt strong and proud of myself. I felt so blessed to be with my mom and dad; to give my sons the family that I so loved and admired. I was making friends and loved being in the classroom. Young people have so much life in them and dream of happiness and a better world. I felt I was where I was supposed to be. I had escaped from hell, and now I wanted to enjoy being alive, with a career, a house, and a life of my own.

One day I was being observed by my UC professor for my clear credential. He sat in the back of the room looking very debonair with his studious glasses, tie and overcoat. My high school class was filled with predominantly teenage boys. Throughout the lesson, one young man was particularly mouthy.

"Justin, you need to settle down."

"Why? What are you going to do about it?"

Bearing straight into his eyes, not changing my voice I said. "Nothing. Just throw you out."

He settled down for a while, but I knew it wasn't over. The lesson continued and the students engaged in the discussion.

I turned to write the next point of the lesson on the board. While my back was turned, Justin said, "Is that why you're dressed all nice? Is that your boyfriend in the back?" I finished writing the example on the board. I had to smile. I knew what he was doing and I liked him for it. My smile disappeared as I turned back around, my eyes stared emotionless into his.

"Get out."

Have you ever had those moments when you know you don't have to succumb to further confrontation just because of the powerful energy of your resolve? Both of us knew that "this" would end now, my way. He made some silly gyrations as he walked out, hoping to provoke me, hoping to get out from under my energy that held him to do as I asked. My eyes held him steadfast.

He became one of my most supportive students, not because he got good grades, but rather, we later included his comments and gyrations as part of the character of our class. And he curbed them to make our dynamics work.

Anything the students, administration, or parents threw at me was a game in comparison to the life I lived with Trip.

Canal Street

A year after I got my first teaching job, my boys and I bought a house. It was an adorable Victorian cottage in the Gold Country. Two bedrooms, two baths, a living room, dining room, a kitchen, breakfast nook and office space. It was a 1906 fixer-upper. Everyday after school I worked on that house. I put in new windows, a wood stove, new kitchen and bathroom. I painted, hung wallpaper and changed fixtures. I loved my life with just my two sons and me. I loved them so much. We had escaped from hell. We had come back to life and we were making a life together.

Missing Piece?

A s time does what it does; pulses on, healing and revealing new desires, I wanted a partner, what I thought then was a complete family. I felt I was missing something. I met Cracker Stacker, Freeway Guy, El Mariachi, Tom, Craig, Channing, and others. I wanted what I had lost with Trip.

In those quiet moments when no one was around to distract me or when I felt tired, overwhelmed or frustrated, I would dwell on the fact that I didn't have a partner to help me, what I had lost, all the burden that I alone carried, that somehow my life wasn't fair. In those moments, I should have redirected my thoughts to the rare love and union my boys and I shared, what I had accomplished on my own or I could have thought about what I wanted and how it would feel to have that and revel in that feeling. Instead, I focused on what I didn't have.

A few years later, I met a history teacher in a credentialing class. He was handsome, tall, quiet yet, confidently charming.

We hit it off and we began to spend our lunch breaks together. One day we went to eat our lunch on the near-by lawn. There was a moment that the conversation ended and instead of trying to fill it with awkward questions or comments, neither of us said a word. It felt so nice, easy, comfortable to just be with him. This was different. We were good for each other for a time. He helped me heal in many ways and we were happy. I was enjoying growing and learning how to love again. My mother, though, with my dad's prompting, kept telling me that I was an unclean woman sleeping with this man without marrying him. I had to make an honest woman of myself, or so I thought. I didn't have the courage, or support nor the understanding to do otherwise. All I saw was that I wanted to create what I thought was a family, not realizing that I had a blessed one already. Also, I didn't want to hurt my mom and dad again.

The next time Trip's parents visited I told them about my love interest.

The three story, redbrick building built in 1857 was where Trip's parents often stayed when they made their once-a-year visit. We sat in the hotel lobby, which was reminiscent of 1857, with Victorian furniture, Tiffany lamps, solid wood beams, and a beautiful carved baluster staircase.

"I have been dating a man and he has asked me to marry him," I told them.

"We knew that this day would come. We didn't think that you would remain single for the rest of your life," she said with a hint of sadness.

"You will always be the boys' grandparents."

"We just want you to have a normal life and not be reminded about the horror you lived with our son," she replied.

"I'd like you to be a part of their lives," I said, not really understanding her response.

I turned my body toward Trip's father, a little annoyed. "Do you have anything to say?" Trip's father looked uncomfortable sitting in a Victorian chair, not because the chair was old and bulky or because he was ashamed of what he was about to say, but rather because he seemed to want to be done with the mishaps of his son. In a cool tone while discreetly looking for his cigar, he said, "I have other grandchildren."

He did not just say that! I thought. It was incomprehensible to me that a person could disregard his offspring as if casting off a cigarette butt. But how could I be shocked? Trip had done it. And his father had done the same to him years before, not physically, but emotionally. These people were sorely mistaken. At that moment, although briefly buffeted by the pain of rejection, again, I felt so lucky. And a blanket of gratitude enveloped my sons and me. I was granted the honor of being the mother of these two precious boys. I knew my sons were special.

But no one is either completely bad or completely good.

Trip had great qualities that I knew I could bring out in Kuder and Tank. Trip taught himself Greek and Hebrew before there was "YouTube University." He had an impeccable work ethic, and pushed himself further than most people. Trip was tender of heart when he was not ridden with guilt and turmoil. Physically, he was very strong and disciplined. He still holds soccer records at Stanford University. I focused on bringing out those good qualities that I knew Kuder and Tank innately had. The three of us had gone through hell and back and I had to help us all to be able to distinguish that our past does not define us, nor do other people, only if we allow it.

The history teacher and I got married one month after the fateful Twin Towers fell, and Trip's family never contacted me nor the boys again.

I was blessed to have two more beautiful sons with this man. This is without a doubt the single most precious gift my second husband gave me. And for that I am forever grateful. My greatest dream was to be a mother. I am so blessed to have four amazing young men in my life. We help each other and love and respect one another deeply. What I have in them is four "pearls of great price."

Seven
Years Later

Family and friends buzz about the house, tasting appetizers, pouring drinks and celebrating Kuder going away to college. "Mama, it feels weird. This is my last meal," he says as he leans into me while he and I are cozily making tortillas for tacos, his favorite dish.

I choke back the emotion. "Only for a while, Mi'jo," I say, concealing a mother's sentimental heart.

In less than twelve hours, I will put Kuder on a plane, entrusting his life into his own hands. *Did I give him the proper tools to become a man? Will our past haunt him? Will he blossom?* These insecurities and more race through my mind as the hours count down to his departure.

I couldn't be more proud as I sense my son's excitement as his dream to study on the East Coast materializes. This is the same boy who failed so many of his classes during his early education, who constantly fought at school and who ultimately pulled himself out of Special Education to finish high school as one of the valedictorians. And now he is attending one of Boston's fine universities. But a primal apprehension wants to hold onto the child I've given my heart and soul to for the last eighteen years. To go separate ways with one of my two sons who lived through and emerged from hell with me, is a difficult thing to do.

4:30 a.m. The dreaded alarm sounds. The time has come to let go.

Still groggy from waking early, we pile into the car, the boys get cozy and go back to sleep.

The airport is still at this hour. We arrive, check his bags and face our goodbyes. Kuder and Tank embrace, knowing they won't see each other for a while. They let go and exchange warm smiles and a handshake. He picks up his two younger brothers and holds them close. He turns to my new husband and they embrace. As they release, my husband whispers something incidental, then offers his hand to shake it. It's my turn. "Can I give you a motherly blessing?"

"Yes, Mama," he says as tenderness covers his face.

We find two inconspicuous wooden chairs in the closed Mrs. Field's cookie shop. We sit face to face with our arms around one another, heads resting on each other's shoulders. "May you have," is all I can say before the tears flow. I try again, still intermittent with tears, but I manage to finish.

"May you have the courage to follow your heart, the humility to always take instruction and the blessing of a life full of love." I kiss his cheek and raise my head to find him wiping his eyes.

We all walk to the escalator where he alone will go through the security checkpoint. He looks back three times, searching my eyes to see if I'm okay, while he sports a satisfied smile that he is on his way to begin his life. We watch as he disappears into the crowd. Tank is by my side. I look into his eyes and see that this moment affects him, too. Kuder and Tank have always been together. Tank has never known life without his brother. The three of us have never lived apart.

Kuder has left my nest. So many emotions race through my veins. Each moment a different winner surfaces between happiness, sorrow, anger, pride, relief. An era so familiar to me is coming to an end and another of unknowns begins. Yet a calm settles over my soul between the alternating eruptions of emotion. I have imparted unto Kuder and Tank all the love, encouragement and guidance I possess in an effort to erase the hell that once haunted us. Once again, I have given all of my being, but this time to my sons from the man I once adored. The responsibility I felt upon their births to raise men, despite my choices, will begin to bear its fruit. Together, we have come far. Now, I must begin to let go. First with Kuder and soon with Tank. I must trust that both won't deny their past, but rather use it to strengthen their character. I must trust this day, as Kuder is the first to leave my nest, that he will be alright, that both my sons will be alright, and that they will create their own legend.

FIN

PART IV

Diamonds
Forged from Fire

It has been almost thirty years since Trip left. And many years have passed since that veil had been drawn back for me to see something I did not understand. Since then, I have sought out priests, pastors, preachers, healers, teachers, psychics, gurus, anyone who would listen; anyone willing to help. I had to make sense of this. But no one gave answers that satisfied me or maybe I just had a difficult time trusting people. It wasn't until recently with much research, study, contemplation, stumbling and action that I realized that the answers are inside of me.

As a young girl, I set out to find truth. After all that has happened and the pain that I have endured, I can say that truth is infinite and unchanging. There are laws embedded in the very fabric of the universe, that when understood and applied, we can be, do, have and give what we want. We are untrained and have blocks, though, that keep us from being, doing, having, and giving whatever we want. Even beyond the blocks, we lack the inner capacity or tools to navigate through them to understand and live by these laws. Like a carpenter with his or her toolbelt, there is a belt that we all need to fill with respective tools so we can create our life deliberately. These tools are interesting because they overlap, go hand in hand and build upon each other. There is no end to their use and expansion. The more they are used, the wider the scope of their ability becomes. These ideas are not mine. I didn't come up with anything, I just uncovered some critical knowledge. As you continue to read, may you hear the truths that made themselves known to me.

Religion

I don't hold stock in religion anymore. I do believe there is a difference between religion and spirituality. Spiritually is a private matter between an individual's perceptions of a greater power and how s/he chooses to revere it. Religion is an institution like any big business whose goal is to increase numbers and revenue, which, in itself, is not a bad thing. The incredible shame is that religion exploits man's innate desire for spirituality for growth and profits in a realm where big business tactics should never be employed. Many religious groups undoubtedly begin with good intentions, but as money and power are in their grasp, the sight of spirituality is lost, and the intricate deception begins.

What if we were taught to be kind to our fellow man because we are creatures of higher thinking and we, unlike animals, possess reason which allows us to choose to respect our neighbor? What we give, we receive. Ultimately, we all want the same things—to have community, to be respected and to have our hearts desires. Instead, we are taught to be kind due to a reward and punishment system. Guilt is a useless motivator. It breeds insincerity and clouds the path to self-discovery and ultimate happiness. Guilt is a great tool for controlling those who choose not to think. Unfortunately, it is used in every realm of human society.

Maybe romanticism and idealism are meant to remain in artistic paintings, beautiful music, uplifting poetry, wondrous books and awe-inspiring dance, not for real life. Maybe it is for the place in our soul where human beings long for it to become reality but for now can only be lived in the world of art; because, as of yet, we haven't achieved a high enough consciousness as a race of people. But individually we can create our world through our imagination and focus. The more vivid the imagery, the faster it becomes real.

Faith of
a Child

It is assumed that a child is not as wise as a parent. Children are far more intelligent and capable than what we adults assume. We adults have lied to ourselves for so long that we then believe our own lies. We first learned to lie from the authority we trusted. When adults teach or discipline a child, the child can see and feel any discrepancy in the eyes and aura of the adult. Children believe because they are pure and full of love and because of this, have faith in authority even over their own innate knowing to the contrary. It is a great responsibility to cultivate the heart of a young one. The most powerful words that initiate greater consciousness in a child are, "I was wrong. I'm sorry. Please forgive me. I love you." You cannot fool the heart of a child. You can, however, fool another adult.

Relationships

The love that maybe comes once in one hundred years came to me. You see the person with all their flaws and short-comings, who he is, and you love him still nonetheless. You would do anything for their happiness and well-being. You are deeply moved by him, not because of social status, looks, money, job, or anything in particular or everything in particular; you just love him.

I have been ridiculed by the people closest to me for having loved Trip so deeply, almost killing me. I am unequivocally thankful for the experience. I was given an immense gift. I felt alive, deeply moved that I had the capacity to love to that extent. Because of it, I saw that the earth is more than what we see and deeper than what is explicable or tangible. It felt amazing! Yet, I am simultaneously heartbroken. Heartbroken that it was not reciprocated. What would it be like to love and to be loved in this way in return? Having only experienced one side of it, I can only imagine that to share it, must border on ecstasy.

I do believe that Trip loved me in the way that he could. I think he felt that I accepted him for the way he was. But the damnable misery is that he did not accept himself. He was never enough and therefore no one could have ever been enough.

You love who you love.

I refuse to allow the pain of my broken heart to dictate how I love another man, to remain jaded or to bring the pain of the past to another. To allow disappointment to curve what I hold as beautiful is what must be earnestly fought against. My journey, in part, includes healing the wounds and sometimes scars of love so as to only bring a bigger heart with the wisdom of its lessons. I try to keep my heart open. Everyone has their own version of love and a relationship. In the end, everyone deserves to be cherished in such a way that s/he feels seen and admired.

The relationship of a child is different from that of a partner. But I love my four sons in this way. If I had had my way, I would have preferred to stay home and homeschool my boys. But, that was not to be. I worked as I raised my boys, for the most part. I made a choice, however, that my priority would be their emotional and psychological well-being above making money or being the best at my job. We all suffered trauma. My boys and I needed help to heal. They, along with me, were experimenting with the truths we were discovering. Again, I am, without qualification, blessed that I have four amazing relationships with my four amazing young men.

Love

Pain is a gift of love. "Love brings up everything unlike itself to be healed," as paraphrased from the book, *A Course in Miracles*. We are love. It is our true essence. When we act in opposition to love, ultimately, there is no peace.

When life didn't turn out the way I thought it should be, I felt something sour, unjust, anger or pain in my being. It came not from the thing that happened, but rather from the story I told myself around what had happened. Usually it was a negative narrative.

Pain must be felt, though. It must be acknowledged. Once I sat with it and figuratively looked into its face, I found a certain comfort there and that is where I met love and understood that love being as it is, brings up all emotions and situations unlike itself to be cleared, taken away. I wasn't being punished. How beautiful!

What if we tried to find the lesson in the pain? And asked ourselves, "What is life trying to show me?"

If we found a lesson and focused on that, maybe we would experience gratitude for the pain that offers the potential growth from that struggle.

Gratitude

I didn't feel in any way grateful for losing my husband and shouldering all the responsibility of a single mother. Honestly, sitting there for two minutes saying, "I'm grateful for losing my husband, being ridiculed for it, made to feel stupid for my choices, feeling like a failure and, oh yeah, and I'm grateful for my shoes."

It seemed a little ridiculous when all I felt was pain. Death seemed easier sometimes because life hurt so much, and I felt I could never get out of all the shit I had created. Nor did I feel that I had the ability or know how, much less the strength to do so. How could I put dust back together?

When I did go through all that had happened and find the pieces for which I could genuinely say I was thankful, it did help. It is easy to be grateful when everything is peachy. It is quite another situation when life presses up against us. Gratitude is an energetic choice. Like all things that we want to master, it must be practiced.

Sometimes the realization of my situation would flood in and I felt how bad it was and it hurt like hell. Sometimes I'd cry, workout, punch a wall, laugh, laugh and cry . . . I had to feel the situation and all its grief for what it was. I learned compassion, too, because sometimes the pain was far too great to face all at once. So I did it in chunks and when I was ready, I could ask: is there good in the mire? In some way, can I look at it differently? This is bad, but maybe it has kept me from something even worse.

We do have the ability to consciously choose how we are going to feel in a given circumstance. Sometimes it seems impossible to do. I realized that I had to feel safe even in my own head, which for me means compassion, love and appreciation for myself. It made it easier to be ready. Then I stopped fighting and released the negative emotions. We are beings of reason and will. It can be done. Having love and compassion for ourselves is key.

Forgiveness

I'm sure you can imagine that I had a difficult time forgiving Trip. I was so angry at him for rejecting us and for all the times he was so unkind. At the end of the day, it was easier to let things go between us. I could see his pain and I could also see how beautiful he was despite all his shortcomings and horrible behavior.

I had a much more arduous time forgiving myself. This was, by far, more damaging to me. *How could I have been so stupid?! So blind?! So naive?! Why didn't I make different choices?! I gave everything of myself, and I got a raw deal. How was this fair?* With all of those thoughts, I was sending destructive messages to myself. I awoke and went to sleep subconsciously living in the energy that I am stupid, blind, unwise, horrible at making decisions and so on. This made it difficult for me to be happy for others in general and those in good relationships and unbroken families. No wonder I lived in a constant state of sadness and disappointment. How could I live from love when this was the perpetuated story?

The problem with forgiveness is that we think that we, as individual human beings, are separate. We forgive because another has offended us. We had nothing to do with the offense.

We cast judgment: they are unworthy and we are worthy. Therefore, we are the gracious ones to offer pardon. But what I did not realize was that we are all one. I judged myself when I judged my offender. What we give to another is what we give to ourselves.

I began to put myself in Trip's shoes. Could I see myself acting the way he did? If I could answer yes, just once, then I was no different. And the responsibility was clear. I have the choice to choose how to respond. It became easier to let go of my resentment toward him and others when I looked at each situation like this.

As for the well-being of others, why wouldn't I want someone else to be happy and not have gone through what I had?

The truth is, we give in many ways, both good and bad. We give physical things, time, energy, emotion, and actions. We also give in thought, which sometimes may be more damaging. What we think in the privacy of our own minds comes to light and takes form eventually. It is reflected back to us. We are all connected, so when I thought thoughts of anger, resentment, strife, etc., I was projecting this kind of life back to myself. To give to another is to give to oneself.

When this truth became evident to me, I consciously began to make a daily effort to be kind to everyone I saw. If I just met someone, in my mind I'd offer peace and success in all their endeavors. Or a couple, I would bless their union or if someone was upset or rude, I'd offer a smile and a compliment to change their disposition. And their attitude changed every time, which is very interesting. It also felt good inside to be this way.

I have to be honest, sometimes I wouldn't have kind feelings toward another. It's not always easy, but the more I practice, the more it becomes obvious that not to do so is detrimental to me. But, like gratitude, it is an energetic choice that I have the ability to make.

Is forgiveness bogus, then, if the only reason I forgive is really for my own benefit? Maybe. When all is said and done, we are all connected, to the earth, to the universe, and to each other.

Boundaries

Forgiveness always seemed to end in being walked on. If I forgave Trip, then that meant that I was okay with how he treated me and my boys. No. A definite hard pass! This is where boundaries are crucial. When I released him for his actions, that's when I felt the chains binding me to my ill feelings in my core loosened, falling to the ground. I was able to walk away without the weight and burden that had been my constant anchor for so many years. But that didn't mean I was willing to put myself back into that situation or condone that behavior.

Our intuition, desire, heart, inner child, or whatever name it is given lives inside of us, but doesn't have a voice, per se. Mine waits for me to defend her and speak on her behalf. She whispers and hopes that I take action accordingly. *Take care of those around you.* That is what I perceived was right. Honestly, I thought that everyone innately would consider his fellow man first. Everyone else came before me because surely I would be considered in return.

With the hard lessons of life came the understanding that we, all, have been hurt by our parents, siblings, extended family, culture, church, society, etc.

You know that situation when something inside says do this, speak up here, declare what you want, but instead you do what you are taught to do because what you're feeling can't possibly be right? I did this. I thought everything was external. And every time I did that, my heart hung her head in dismay. The truth is that everything is internal first. So boundaries are necessary to awaken our friends, family and lovers so that they can see who we really are, that we are not afraid to be seen, and we realize that we are good enough, skilled enough, educated enough, old enough, young enough, whatever enough.

Do not confuse selfishness with boundaries. Having boundaries is recognizing what our heart wants and having the courage to respond to its desires, either with words or actions. It is deliberate. We put forth a more authentic person which creates clarity for those around us and strength and compassion for ourselves. How can we really honor another if we first don't honor ourselves? When we don't do this, we present ourselves as someone we are not.

Failure

For years I had been hung up on the fact that my marriage to Trip failed. I had failed in the worst way possible in one of life's paths that I most wanted. No matter how I looked at it, I failed and I was ashamed. With time, contemplation and practice, I came to understand that failure is nothing more than information. What information could I gather about my supposed, "failure?" Well, I could look at my marriage as a failure; afterall, I did attempt something, and it didn't work. But I could also look at it as information to use going forward. What aspects made me feel like a failure? How could I turn them around to feel something I could accept? I saw what I didn't want. What is it that I did like? Want? And I learned compassion for myself; for doing the best that I could with the information that I had at that time and to forgive myself for not getting it, supposedly, right. Then again, what is "right" other than a preordained standard given to me by another.

I felt empowered looking at my marriage and supposed mistakes from this point of view. And I felt free, unpunished by that word, "failure," because in reality, there is no such thing as failure. It's the energy that we put into a situation that makes it become what it becomes. either something negative, something positive or a combination thereof.

Fear

When I speak of fear, I'm not talking about the feeling when the hair on the back of your neck stands up and there's a sense of danger about. The fear I am talking about here is the fear of failing, the fear of not being good enough, skilled enough, educated enough, old enough, young enough, whatever enough. The feelings that bring up all the excuses as to why *it* won't work or *it* can never happen.

Fear is like a rose. Each petal is a different fear. These petals surround the seed, the beautiful being inside, protecting it. When someone is ready to release a fear, or is tired of being afraid of that particular thing, that fear is gone. As the true being begins to stand erect, reaching for the limitless, the petals of fear fall away, back to the earth. Fear is really love protecting the unfurling being until and *if* s/he is ready to come into his/her self. This type of fear stands at the threshold of becoming who we are meant to be.

I began to look at my fears from the perspective of an outsider looking in. Logically, these fears make no sense. I am enough! As I contemplated these fears further, I uncovered feelings that I had been holding about myself that most of the time I didn't even realize I had. But where did this self-concept of me come from? My belief of who I am and what I can accomplish came from the stories I created that were rooted in my upbringing, culture, society, and education.

Without proper understanding, it's very difficult to discern who we really are amongst the onslaughts of our surroundings. It wasn't until I began to comprehend that we are greater than just the body, that we are part of the infinite experiencing a human life, and that there is far more to us than what we presently believe. As I experiment with this information, the power of my fears waver in the strength of knowing.

Responsibility

It took me a long time to grasp this one. As with all principles though, I'm still grasping. At different times, I made excuses for my pain, loss or misfortune. I blamed people, circumstances, situations, society, upbringing, you name it. And it felt good in some way. But in doing so, I was constantly fighting nothing. Little did I know that I was expending energy that could have been better spent; like thinking on a life I wanted instead of blaming, making excuses or comparing. Alas, this is part of grieving. We have to be honest with how we feel, but the key is not to stay there.

Like someone shaking me from a deep sleep, I awoke, opened my eyes and realized that it is me and only me that thinks and feels what I think and feel and that, my thoughts and emotions are in my control to navigate. No one else can think and feel for me. I stopped my pity-party.

The Sacred Feminine /
The Sacred Masculine

If you are feminine and a woman, there is great beauty and power in that. Femininity does not equate to weakness. Nor does a strong woman equate to she who acts like a man. Femininity is compassion, clear, strength in endurance, unwavering in persistence, intuitive, supportive, and unyielding. I don't know if I would call myself a feminist because I equally think that there is great power and beauty in the sacred masculine. Masculine energy has the desire to protect and provide, and is drawn to action, decisive and logical, and has many of the same qualities as those considered feminine.

I have raised four boys. Each son is very different from his brothers. I have noticed that each of my sons, as well as myself, all have these qualities innately to varying degrees. At the end of the day, it's about embracing the masculine or feminine expression that we are and cultivating a mixture of these seemingly opposing qualities in our female or male body in such a way that expresses who we feel we truly are inside.

It is something quite beautiful and attractive to meet a man or woman who has embraced and embellished their sacredness in the female or male form.

Kuder told me recently,

"Mama, I am a man raised by a woman."

It has taken years to undo the brainwashing of Trip's cultish manipulation and of his ill-respect of women. Gratefully, I now rest knowing he was sadly mistaken on so many levels. Yet, I have deep compassion for him because he was reacting out of great internal pain, and he didn't have the understanding nor the inner capacity to change his destiny.

Attention

When something or someone is a treasure to us, we are always thinking about it. It can be the house we want to buy, a job we want, a goal, travel plans, a person. Even events like getting a bad health diagnosis, fired, divorced, or losing someone dear to us. Our hearts are filled with emotion around it. The treasure can either be good or bad. Good: I am so in love with this person. Bad: why did this happen to me??? It does not matter in the mind. What matters is the amount of thoughts and emotion centered around it. Therefore, think about what you want, not about what you have.

Through our thoughts, we create life. Life is thought.

Essence

Everyone of us is beautiful. With some people we jive, with others not so much, but does that make those with whom we don't align less beautiful? We are 100 percent love, trying to recognize this in our human experience. To make mistakes, cause pain, make love, and bring joy are all part of the process of this recognition.

The Rockies

A lthough my time with Trip was dark and disheartening, I have deep gratitude for the region of the Rockies. We spent all our years together jumping from place to place around the three states that cradle Yellowstone. Even now, when I see a picture of Montana and her majestic mountains, smell the fall breeze rustle through an aspen grove, or hear a tune that played when we lived there, I am reminded of how deeply touched I am by Mother Earth and those years we spent protected by her grandeur. I long to know her more deeply.

Kuder and Tank

You might be wondering where Kuder and Tank are in life and how they fare. Kuder has spent time on all seven continents of this planet before he turned thirty. He went on to get his PhD in plasma physics. He is now working on nuclear fusion. Tank has spent time abroad as well. He is now living in Iceland, working as a self-taught software engineer. He is also a musician, singer, dancer and permaculture enthusiast.

As you know, we have had our difficulties, but if you were to meet us now, you would never have guessed that we were the ones who came out of Hell. I must say, though, that we are not perfect, we just keep doing and contemplate the truths that made themselves known.

Death–What If?

Ihave never understood death. I know what I am supposed
to know. It's the cycle of life and all. But the pain of the loss
doesn't make sense to me.

Practice gratitude, practice forgiveness, practice kindness,
because these attributes vibrate on the same frequency of love,
so therefore, if we practice them, we will attract positive things
to our lives. And it works. These practices are like the precursor
to the road to discovering who we really are. The quest, then, is
to find out who we really are. However, no one ever really arrives
because we are infinite and infinite are the ways we can grow
and expand. So if we live eighty to a hundred years and some of
us, way less than that, it hardly seems like a proper opportunity
to even begin to understand and discover our true essence. We
barely begin. Most of us never really begin. So it seems so unfair
to live such a short lifespan. We live and die never discovering
the truth about ourselves.

And another thought: if we create our lives by what we con-
tinually think, fueled with emotion and imagery, then we could
create a life we love and if we can create a life we love, could we
create away disease? If we could create away illness, then what
about aging? Death? What if we age, get sick and die, only

because collectively that is what we all believe? What if it is our choice? What if we are supposed to give up this life when we feel it is time to leave this body and go on to what comes next?

However, the longer we live on this earth the way we, as a collective, think now, the longer we live without love. The years drain away the hope and love with which we started. We become bitter from our mistakes, losses, and unrealized dreams. We walk further away from our true essence and the will to live diminishes. We are disheartened. Why wouldn't we summon death as we grow older and create ways to "get out?"

Life is thought. We are love. What is life without love?

Manifestation

I hesitate, don't commit or act upon a dream because I do not trust the source from which I heard the inspiration. The inspiration comes from within conditioned by beliefs.

Listen to people who have what I want to learn how they achieved their goals that are similar to mine. But even after I have what I want, a yearning remains. Listening to people who have what I want is intellect, but there is a deeper part of me that I must listen to just as intently. I am more than just the physical; I am spirit.

Within all of us there is a source that goes by many names; spirit, soul, God, energy, love, universe, etc. This is the source from which all things come. It's not the mind, it's not the body. The mind and the body are tools that this source uses. It is from this source that we can create miracles or a life we want.

We create from who we are.

So if we don't believe we deserve what we dream of achieving, that is what we create. We create a lesser version of the dream or something else entirely, justifying our lack of deservingness while focusing on the fact that we have what we don't want and can't have, perpetuating this negative cycle.

If we believe we deserve whatever it is we long for, then we create what we long for. If we've had a blessed life or come from a blessed family it's easy to believe that we can create a blessed life. Some of us just can't believe that we deserve the things we want because of the many manifestations of trauma that we have experienced. It is difficult to believe that we can create other than more of the same, so we create more of the same. If we knew we were love, we would know we are worthy.

Whether we believe we are from favor or from trauma, the bottom line is that we all come from the same source, which is love. Love cancels everything unlike itself because we are not that. We have taken on everything other than love from the conditioning around us.

The missing piece is knowing who we really are and where we come from. We are love and we come from love. How do we know this? It is in our hearts. In order to rediscover it, we must reconnect with Mother Earth, still the inner chatter, and follow our intuition. Although it seems simple, each suggestion is far reaching and profound. It takes will, perseverance and practice and must be done individually to affect us collectively.

The law of attraction does not work for everything or for everyone because we create from who we believe we are not from who we really are.

We take action because we believe. We stop taking action because we have lost sight of what we believed. And what we believe is who we are.

When you get discouraged, the road is difficult, or you're tired, forget about it. Go do something that brings even a glint of relief. Find the thing that comes to your mind that makes you feel just a little bit better and go do it.

If we manifest who we are, how do we change who we are to manifest the life we want? We can't change who we are; we can only find out who we are.

Jesus

The Jesus that leapt out the window in my darkest hour so many years ago, was the Jesus of my own creation. The validity of my belief in him, religion, about how life works, failed when I needed real power. Truth can never fail. How could that Jesus have helped? He was not real. I created him from the beliefs that I gathered from my culture, society, and religion.

I have come to understand that the true Jesus is an Ascended Master. He didn't come to create a religion. He came to teach us what we inherently are and to understand and use the abilities we all innately have. Even now he is accessible to help us on our own journey. He is not the hero, though. Each of us is the hero of our own story. Don't wait for someone to do it for you or give you a quick fix. We all must take responsibility for our lives.

Dust cannot be reassembled, nor can our lives when they fall apart. They must be made all together new from our will and new understanding, which is gathered and applied from beneath the rubble of our seeming destruction.

All those years ago, when the veil was opened and pulled back for me to see the uncertainties upon which our present society stands, I received the most gracious gift. It was the doorway onto this path of discovery: love, upon which all exists. This is only the beginning.

My Teachers

I have always associated teachers to be those with whom I have had personal contact. But now, not so much. I have yet to meet a real person. Every teacher I have had, I met through books, audio or Zoom. I must give thanks to all the people who have given me bits and pieces to the puzzle of life. Energetically, you know who you are. Some are alive, others are found in the pages of history and still others, you could say, are out of this world. My greatest and dearest teacher, though, has been and continues to be this experience we call Life. Forgiveness lives in each of us, which is hope, which is joy, which is peace, which is sight, which is force, which is Love, which is God. You and I are never alone, nor ever have been or ever will be.

Life Force

The force that drew me into religion is the same force that made me overcome religion, overcome my darkest despair and devastation. It is the force that begs me not to give up. It is the same force that draws me to write this book, which is the same force that brings me to you.

I bless you for reading my words. May all the good that you ever want come your way. If I may leave you with one principle by which to live your life, it is this: feel your heart and follow it to become who you are meant to be. Your heart whispers, it does not yell, so become familiar with this still voice; your dearest of friends. There is tremendous joy in living the life you know you were meant to live. You truly come alive and become a powerful force.

Avoid doing what you are "supposed to do" or what is expected of you. It's not always that easy, I know. It takes true valor to feel your heart and follow it. Remember, you have what it takes. Otherwise you wouldn't be on this earth. I remind myself of these words, as well. So follow your heart, because the world needs the real you. You already know this, your heart yearns for you.

We are all on a journey. Peace to you, my fellow traveler. I leave you in Love.

Love, Lydia

Acknowledgements

I could not have done this project alone. First, I'd like to thank my four sons for their faith in me through everything and for being my biggest supporters. To my friends and family for their excitement and encouragement. To Nora Profit, thank you for all your help in the early stages of this book. To Jennifer Basye Sander and Writers Who Wine. To Jack Canfield for his keen suggestion. Thank you to my First Readers: JB, CK, CW and JIS, JDS, WSE and TSE. To my production team at the Steve Harrison group. To all the coaches at GPN. These people have been amazing. All the elements of producing a book would have been one hundred times more difficult if it were not for them. To Debby Englander, you have been my angel, thank you! Thank you to Christina Smith, for keeping us all on plan. To Valerie Costa for her expertise. To Christy Day for her cover art, book interior design and patience. To Steve Scholl and Maggie McLaughlin for their expertise. I'd also like to thank the publicity team; Geoffrey Berwind, Danette Kubanda, Nick Summa, Brad Segall, Mary Giuseffi and so many others for their prowess and guidance. There is so much more than meets the eye in writing and producing a book. To everyone, thank you from my full heart to yours.

Love, Lydia

About the Author

 Lydia Gascón Samaniego is the author of *To Hell With You: An Adventure Through Tragedy, Love, Betrayal and Transformation.* Lydia is a woman of hope who believes anything can be overcome. She is a teacher, yoga enthusiast, energy and sound bath practitioner and life coach. She studied at USC and Universidad de Salamanca in Spain. For more about Lydia, speaking engagements and interviews visit, lydiasamaniego.com. Lydia is the mother of four young men and lives in the Sierra Nevada Mountains near Lake Tahoe California. Lydia enjoys time with family and friends, dancing, singing, hiking, gardening, natural medicine, the great outdoors and human potential.

www.ingramcontent.com/pod-product-compliance
Lightning Source LLC
Chambersburg PA
CBHW070707130626
46553CB00005B/1879